Divine Technology: Harnessing AI for a Christ-Centered Life

With the acceleration of technology, a new era has dawned in this world where humans are already mixing with the artificial intelligence (AI) that surpasses all the previous and fictitious ones. Our society has shifted to one where AI is intertwined into everything from our communicative and learning methods, to how we work, worship and play. Christians need to find out how to bring a Christ-centred paradigm to a world where AI is being used so rapidly to expand our lives.

DR. Selva Sugunendran

CEng, MIEE, MCMI, CHt, MIMDHA, MBBNLP, MGONLP, DBS
AI Robotics Strategist & Visionary Author
#1 Best Selling Author, Speaker & Coach
Website: https://AIRoboticsForGood.com
Email: Selva@AIRoboticsForGood.com
AI BOOKS: https://selvasmail.com/selvasbooks

Book Titles

Each title attempts to distil the book's manifesto – helping young people take over AI, indeed take over the future.

Hello & Welcome!

If you have been looking at the title of the book, let me say, any of the following titles would apply to the contents of this book:

How should the emerging and rapidly evolving field of AI be used for the benefit of humankind? This is a question that I have devoted considerable time and brainpower to, and like Paul under the burning sun on the road to Damascus, I cannot unsee nor unhear the call: that technology has the potential to be a transformative force, one that can help bypass humanity's obstinate lapses into sinfulness. With technology, we could truly build the Kingdom of God. Why? Because properly harnessed, and in line with an ethical framework, technology can be exceedingly useful.

"Faith and Innovation: Embracing AI to Deepen Your Walk with God"

"Divine Technology: Harnessing AI for a Christ-Cantered Life"

"AI and the Kingdom: Using Technology to Serve and Grow in Faith"

"Christian Wisdom in the Age of AI: Balancing Faith and Technology"

"Spiritual Growth in a Digital World: AI as a Tool for Christian Living"

About The Book

"Divine Technology: Harnessing AI for a Christ-Centered Life"

With profound joy and enthusiastic commitment, I hereby present to you, *"Divine Technology: Harnessing AI for a Christ-Centered Life"*

I am a born-again Christian and an AI Robotics Strategist. I spent the best part of my professional career of more than 10 years at the nexus of faith and technology. How should the emerging and rapidly evolving field of AI be used for the benefit of humankind? This is a question that I have devoted considerable time and brainpower to, and like Paul under the burning sun on the road to Damascus, I cannot unsee nor unhear the call: that technology has the potential to be a transformative force, one that can help bypass humanity's obstinate lapses into sinfulness. With technology, we could truly build the Kingdom of God. Why? Because properly harnessed, and in line with an ethical framework, technology can be exceedingly useful.

I have written seven books on AI and robotics during my career. Each of these books demystified the topic and presented ideas about how society can learn to use AI effectively. This book has a special focus because its application relates to how we will use this new technology, perhaps the most important technology in that it relates to our faith journey and our relationship with God.

Never before, Christians had to engage so thoughtfully and pre-emptively with technological advancements - an advancement that is no longer abstract or far-away. Rather, AI is with us all the time, shaping how we communicate, work, do ministry, worship and live. We are called to be in the world but not of it.

'Divine Technology: Harnessing AI for a Christ-Cantered Life' is a timely and in-depth guide to using AI to enhance our relationship with God, our worship, our ministries and our everyday lives. It provides practical guidance on how we might use AI to help guide us and others toward the truth and claims of the gospel, including in ethically complex situations. It also carefully considers the rights, dignity and privacy of others.

As I have described elsewhere, AI and robotics technologies can be transformative, they can help solve technical challenges, and they can make the world healthier, happier, better educated and more prosperous. But they will do so only if we harness them in a thoughtful way – that is, if we root them in ethical commitments and use them to express the love, justice and mercy that underpin the Christian worldview. This book shows the way for Christians who want to wield AI without giving up on Christ.

Another appealing feature of the book is its balance, encouraging readers 'to welcome the opportunities and to acknowledge the challenges that may come with them.' I do not wish to duck the hard questions, but I do encourage my readers to dive into those matters honestly and in prayer, while offering such recourses as Bible study questions discussions, online resources and prayers for ministry and pastoral leadership (there are also specific resources for parents and teens, discussion questions for book clubs, as well as an extensive bibliography and exercises for individual readers). Whether you're a pastor or ministry leader seeking tools, a parent, teen or believer hoping to understand how to navigate issues in the digital age, this volume will provide solid facts and places from which to think about God-honouring uses of AI in your life and those of those entrusted to your care and leadership.

I am a Visionary Author and a strategist in AI and robotics, and what I'm trying to say is that the future is not something we passively walk into, it's something we build; this book is an invitation for Christians across the world to build the future of AI in the way that I believe we should – one that is constituted by values born out of our faith; to be leaders in the ethical use of technology; to be innovators in applying AI to the spiritual life; to be – in very real words today – a witness for the power of God in a world that is increasingly driven by data and algorithms.

I pray that you will share my passion for this topic, and that you will read more books to understand the intersections of faith and technology. Those who approach AI with an open mind can be rewarded. They might discover that, instead of competing with God, AI can lead us closer to the divine. It might enable us to serve others with our strengths and compensate for our weaknesses. And it might enable us to be the hands and feet of Jesus while enjoying the benefits of modern living.

I hope that reading, "Divine Technology: Harnessing AI for a Christ-Centered Life" will inspire you to embrace that journey with an openness of heart, as you contemplate how AI can become a key component of your spiritual life, and as you anticipate how your faith in Christ's res- urrection can and will ensure that a Christ-centred life will be the highest goal of AI's evolution. Let us move forward together, knowing that the risen Christ will move us forward, harnessing AI to illuminate the ways of God's Kingdom here on Earth.

In Christ's service,

DR. Selva

(AI Robotics Strategist and Visionary Author)

About The Author

DR SELVA SUGUNENDRAN has performed many lofty positions in life, The most uplifting to him is the one he chose, which was to serve mankind by showing them the way to health, wealth, and success.

Upon selling his UK based Integrated High Security IT company which he ran for 25 years as the company owner, he took the "jump" out of the corporate world into his passion for helping people to be more, do more and get more out of their life than they ever thought possible! Young or old, he helped them create a new blueprint for life that literally changed their world and continues to do so.

As a result of that work, he was attracted to study, research, write and publish 50+ books of which 6 books were #1 Best Sellers in genres Health & Wellness, Alzheimer's / Dementia, Success in Business &Life, and Christianity & more recently on AI & Robotics.

He has developed a special Ai- Robotic Machine (which is currently in a prototype stage) which can be used as a "Virtual Carer" for Dementia patients who live alone and cannot afford 24-hour care.

His books on Ai were prepared for people who are NOT experts on AI, so that they can learn about AI and Robotics, the power of AI as well as pros and cons including ethical considerations.

The current book is a timely and in-depth guide to using AI to enhance our relationship with God, our worship, our ministries and our everyday lives. It provides practical guidance on how we might use AI to help guide us and others toward the truth and claims of the gospel, including in ethically complex situations. It also carefully considers the rights, dignity and privacy of others.

Contents

Here are 16 chapters focussed on the theme that technology has the potential to be a transformative force, one that can help bypass humanity's obstinate lapses into sinfulness. With technology, we could truly build the Kingdom of God. Why? Because properly harnessed, and in line with an ethical framework, technology can be exceedingly useful.

Here you go!

Introduction

"Divine Technology: Harnessing AI for a Christ-Cantered Life"

With the acceleration of technology, a new era has dawned in this world where humans are already mixing with the artificial intelligence (AI) that surpasses all the previous and fictitious ones. Our society has shifted to one where AI is intertwined into everything from our communicative and learning methods, to how we work, worship and play. Christians need to find out how to bring a Christ-centred paradigm to a world where AI is being used so rapidly to expand our lives.

The book, "Divine Technology: Harnessing AI for a Christ-Cantered Life" tackles this question and provides a concrete roadmap for how we can incorporate AI into spiritual life, leadership, ministry and daily living. In a society where practicing one's faith is central to life, AI offers unique digital opportunities and risks, in areas of personal spiritual growth and worship, leading congregations and ministering to fellow human beings, preaching the Gospel, evangelising, and communicating more broadly about faith.

The Intersection of Faith and Technology

This exploration begins from an assumption that it is your duty in Christ not only to lead but also to 'warmly embrace' modern technological advancements such as AI. For we are called to be 'in the world, but not of the world' (John 17:14-16), and, as modern Christians, we must learn to engage with our world, and the technology that shapes it, in forms appropriate to our faith and honouring to God.

The entanglement of religion and technology is nothing new. Christians continually adapt the faith to new technological realities, from the printing press that opened the Bible to a wider audience to the radio and television that broadcast the Gospel to all the inhabited world. Artificial intelligence marks the latest iteration of that evolution. Alongside tremendous opportunities to understand Scripture better, to worship more effectively and to extend the reach and impact of ministry and evangelism, though, AI also introduces ethical hazards and liabilities that must be addressed.

Understanding AI: Friend or Foe?

Our ability to effectively interact with AI largely depends on how we think about it, distinguishing what it can and cannot do, and what it is and isn't. Artificial intelligence (AI) is a collection of technologies designed to make machines behave in ways we would also consider intelligent. This means anything from learning from data or recognising patterns to making decisions or having conversations. AI is built into so many tools we use every day, from smartphone assistants or algorithms behind social media feeds to more complex uses such as predictive analytics or autonomous systems.

However, power brings with its accountability. AI is neither inherently good nor inherently bad – it is a technology that has uses, for good and evil, depending on the intent of those who build and employ it. For Christians, our task is to see that it is employed consistent with the ends intended by the biblical God – with respect for justice, human dignity and communal flourishing. This requires agility, good judgment and a firm grasp of what AI has to offer – and what it does not.

The Role of AI in a Christ-centred Life

One of the central themes of the book is how AI might fit within a Christian life, to be integrated into spiritual practices, building on (rather than supplanting) current ways we've been guided in those spiritual practices. AI-generated tools can help us remain more accountable and intentional in cultivating regular forms of devotion to Christ, such as creating personalised Bible study plans, prayer-based guidance, and prompts to be aware of God's presence throughout the day, as we practice important spiritual disciplines that help us remain oriented to Jesus.

Furthermore, AI might strengthen ministry and community within churches and Christian organisations by revealing needs of congregations and designing tailored outreach, and even better budgeting. Evangelism can reach new audiences with boundaries largely restricted by language, culture and geography. It is essential that the relational or communal element of all that we do for God is maintained, with technology enhancing rather than detracting from the message of Christ.

Navigating Ethical Challenges

A realisation that, as much as AI brings blessings, there are also grave ethical questions at stake In Chapter 4 – 'The Rise of Artificial Intelligence: Ethical and Theological Challenges' – the book outlines some of the ethical questions around AI, including the possibility of AI being used as a tool for 'automated surveillance'. Among the ethical concerns are issues related to privacy, data security, bias, and the use of AI to 'dehumanise' the 'human-to-human' interactions. Christians, says the chapter, must play a proactive role in demanding ethical AI practices that protect 'human rights and dignity'. The book concluded with suggestions about how to 'examine whether uses of AI in our life and in society [are] conducive for justice, fairness, and love'.

It's precisely because of these challenges that Christian community and leadership are so important. Through dialogue, learning from one another, and holding each other accountable, we can ensure that our use of AI is shaped by the person of Christ. This book prompts readers to consider the implications of AI in their spiritual lives, and to find ways to use the technology in ways that remain honourable before God.

A Journey of Faith and Technology

It is this kind of pilgrimage of faith and technology that all who read this book will take, from developing an AI incarnation of Jesus to training robots to serve as community chaplains; from the digital Jesus on our phones to the God we worship on our knees. May it equip us with a Heideggerian spirit and Socratic patience to take the risks of innovation while keeping the Gospel beacons lit. May it inspire a vision of human and spiritual flourishing through AI that eventually will lead us to audio-visual holograms of the risen Lord. And may it be accomplished through our dependence upon prayerful discernment and the Holy Spirit.

In this book, I want to help you foster compassion for the persons behind AI, the technologies involved in it, and the audiences experiencing them. From today forward, my hope is that you have the motivation and resources to critically and Christ-like stand with the marginalised to address the wrongs of surveillance capitalism. You need to read this book because you are a pastor. You need to read this book because you are a leader of a ministry. You need to read this book because you are a parent. You need to read this book because you are any kind of believer. You need to read this book especially if you want to learn how to use AI to the glory of God and the expansion of his Kingdom.

Happy trails to you on this frontier and may you both seize the day by the possibilities that AI brings to us, as well as watch the day for the dangers that AI will bring to our culture. May faith leaders not hastily dismiss how technology can be a blessing to us, and the world, keeping our eyes constantly on Jesus, 'the author and finisher of our faith' (Hebrews 12:2).

(This introduction serves as the thematic and conceptual table of contents for the book, laying out the major topics and issues in integrating AI into Christ-centred life and ministry. It invites you to consider and embrace the opportunities and responsibilities of deploying AI to further the Christian cause of spiritual growth, ministry and evangelism.)

CHAPTER ONE

The Intersection of Faith and Technology: A New Era for Believers

Throughout the history of technology, faith and technology seem to have kept a certain distance from each other. It can feel like we keep shuttling between the different worlds of technology and the world of the faith that we hold so dear. AI escalates the tension between the Christian faith and the continued and undeniable progress of technology. In this chapter, I want to consider some of the areas where AI intersects with the Christian faith and shares some tools that we believers can use to thoughtfully and wisely navigate this brave new technological world with Christ at its centre.

A Historical Perspective: Faith and Technology

Presumably, they will have their hands full as technological innovations roll out that disrupt society even more radically than all those that have come before. Christians have always had to confront new technological advances. When the printing press appeared in the West, it ended up putting a copy of God's Word in the hands of more than a few anonymous simpletons. In fact, it made the Bible available to people who up till then had been stuck at the level of illiteracy. Radio and television broadcast new voices into living rooms around the world. Each time, at first conservative voices warned of the dangers of the new technology, but eventually inspired enthusiasts discovered how to use it in ways that glorified their God. More often than not, these simultaneous exhortations to run and recommendations not to walk covered some pretty utilitarian but unglamorous ground.

Today we face this process anew as AI stands as the latest technological 'tool' that must be vetted and assessed in light of the questions that arise during the process: Will AI machines be seen merely as 'instruments' that we use to gain knowledge and advance a greater good, or might they be recognised as devices that have the potential to learn, grow, adapt and even make judgments of their own? How does the nature of AI affect our work and discernment about how we are to use this technology to further God's creative purposes in the world and address the needs and cries of God's people amid today's research and development?

The Opportunities AI Presents for Christians

There are many ways that AI can benefit our Christian discipleship. Perhaps one of the most immediate is how AI can search and process data in a timely and accurate manner so that Christians can connect with the Bible in ways they couldn't or wouldn't before. What might have taken hours or days to discover through traditional study techniques can be discovered in a matter of minutes or seconds if aided by AI. For instance, Bible study tools that have been aided by AI can help provide insights and connections within Scripture (eg, cross-referenced biblical texts), as well as historical context and applications for our lives today.

A second, potentially exciting application is evangelism. Christians could harness AI to study patterns in social media to help them target their outreach more efficiently. Imagine an AI that interrogated Google searches to find people who were looking for an answer to their prayers or help when questioning their purpose in life and who, therefore, might get traction from Gospel material couched in the answers to their specific questions.

AI could also serve an important role in ministry in places where human resources are hard to come by, such as providing prayer or counselling on demand 24/7 for those seeking answers, help, prayer, or just a few words of encouragement. AI chatbots could help connect people in crisis to the right resources, supplying comfort in their moments of need. Though such AI-driven interactions will never be as effective or emotionally succinct as human-to-human ministry, they could be an effective complement. This is helpful especially in large congregations or remote communities.

The Challenges AI Brings to Our Faith

Indeed, the possibilities are very exciting, but we must also reckon with the problems. The most important is how we use it ethically as Christians, and what kinds of uses can fall short of God's expectations or might even violate them. AI is a very powerful technology. This is why technological determinism (the theory that technology drives everything) can certainly hold water, implying the need for a robust ethics of artificial intelligence (AI). There are current applications of AI that prioritise profit above people: many algorithms promote exploitation, discrimination and human rights violations.

A final danger is that the Cross will continue to become a distant armchair for us during these end times where we must those who have had their spiritual horizon expanded by tapping into the psalmist's ancient technology of the imagination.

Furthermore, the rise of AI raises questions of deep theological import. What is man or woman? What does it mean to be human at a time when machines can think and act in ways not unlike others with the same potential? What understanding of those with whom we walk upon this earth when we cannot tell the 'good bots' from the 'bad', or when bots can become programme authors writing algorithms concerning algorithms? These are questions for theological thinking and changes in pastoral ministry that theologians and Christian leader must addressed. This is only the beginning of the AI age.

Navigating the AI Era with a Christ-Cantered Focus

As we pursue the promise of AI, may we do so Theo-centrically, in the name of Christ, recognising that God gathers, empowers, integrates and enables creation in ways consistent with his character and service to him and his Kingdom. May critical theological thinking and life enable us, as we call on the Lord to enrich our faith, to lead us in the paths embodied by the role of Christ – that we may be more Christian by opening wide the possibilities that exist while creating a path toward Christ and his Kingdom that keeps us rooted in Him.

We can maintain this focus – and perhaps the social rituals that sustain it – by setting boundaries on our use of AI: for example, by being disciplined about our use of technology, including unplugging and dedicating time to prayer, Bible study and fellowship with other Christians at various points each week. Most generally, we can reflect on how to use artificial intelligence in a way that advances rather than conflicts with our higher calling in Christ.

Accountability: We demand it in other aspects of Christian discipleship, so why not here? It might mean having an accountability partner with whom you can check in about your tech habits. It could be a spiritual director or other Christian friend. Or you might form a small group in church or another Christian community to talk through some of these issues together.

AI is no longer a fleeting technology of the future. For better or worse, it's here, and it's an expansive enterprise only going to impact and change every aspect of life for the foreseeable future. As Christians, we have an opportunity to both pay attention to and interact with AI carefully and deliberately, putting it to work for good in our lives, formed by the Christian faith and committed to Christ in all that we do. It won't always be easy, but like everything else in life, when we stay focused on Jesus, we'll get there.

CHAPTER TWO

Understanding AI: What Every Christian Needs to Know

I f like me, you've probably heard the term artificial intelligence (AI) bandied about quite a bit in recent conversation. But what exactly is AI? If you're like most people, you might think it's something that sounds a long way off, something for futurists and tech visionaries. Or maybe for people in the field of science. But in an ever-increasingly sci-fi world, Christians need to have at least a foundational understanding of what AI is and how it works. It's the goal of this chapter to help you understand AI on a basic level, a level that will allow you to explore the rest of this book and the concepts found in it with more proficiency and understanding.

Defining Artificial Intelligence

Fundamentally, Artificial Intelligence refers to the ability of machines to imitate characteristics of human activities normally associated with intelligence, such as reasoning, learning from examples, problem-solving,

Perceiving information from the environment, and understanding or generating human-sounding text (human linguistic communication). AI can vary from simple applications (like your mobile phone's virtual assistant) to more sophisticated systems (such as autonomous vehicles or analysis tools), for example.

We typically divide AI into two types: narrow AI, which is made to do a particular computational task such as recognising faces or translating languages, and is great at that task, but can't do anything else; and "General AI", which would in principle be able to accomplish any of the intellectual tasks that a human agent is capable of doing – the type of AI with which we might get ourselves into a world of trouble. We're mostly in the theoretical realm regarding general AI. Much of the AI we currently employ, mostly narrow AI, operates at the levels of perceiving, saving, accessing, computing and reproducing information.

How AI Works: The Basics

But to gain a simplified understanding of how this works, some basic principles can help. At the heart of an AI is an algorithm, a series of codified rules that a computer follows to complete some tasks. When you interact with an AI system, your data is collected and processed according to its set of rules so that the system can generate decisions or predictions based on your inputs.

Probably its biggest strength is that it can learn – the process of which is generally based on **machine learning**, a branch of AI where these kinds of systems get better at solving tasks the more data they are given. For example, starting with hundreds of thousands of emails classified as 'spam' or 'not spam', you could train an email filtering machine learning algorithm to improve how it performs its task as it's exposed to more emails.

A more sophisticated form of machine learning, however, is a type of artificial intelligence described using the term **deep learning**, which involves neural networks – models based on the human brain – with layers upon layers, enabling such systems to discover more and more complex patterns within the information it processes. Deep learning is responsible for some of the most exciting new AI achievements over the past decade, such as sight recognition and speech.

AI in Everyday Life

AI can seem like a futuristic idea, but it's all around us in ways that we might not realise. If you've ever used Siri or Alexa on your phone, if Netflix or Amazon suggests a new film you'd like to watch, or if you rely on Google Maps to explore a city, chances are you've interacted with artificial intelligence. Its presence in everyday life makes your life easier, but it also raises important questions about privacy, ethics and technological dependency.

For those of us who follow Christ, acknowledging the all-encompassing role of AI in our lives is the beginning of the path toward harnessing it responsibly. AI can be a boon to humanity, but it can also steer the hearts and minds of users in ways that hinder us from acting compassionately with one another. For instance, social media algorithms that rely on AI and machine learning are optimised to catch our attention. They often accomplish this goal by showing us articles and videos that affirm pre-existing convictions or resonate with emotions. This creates echo chambers for the ideas we are exposed to, enabling us to interact only with those who agree with us on certain issues or buy into our current set of beliefs. The constructive relationships that Jesus sought to foster were built in the in-between spaces shared with those unlike us; they were fostered with neighbours, sceptics and heroes alike.

The Ethical Implications of AI

Concerns centred around the ethics of decisions made by AI systems are one of the most immediate concerns surrounding the exponential development of AI. Given that AI systems can become increasingly involved in decision-making processes, particularly as more autonomous systems ability continues to expand, individuals begin to question whether these systems can be held accountable for their decisions. Additionally, they will want to know how they can bend these algorithms towards or away from outcomes reflective of social justice. For example, hiring and lending AI algorithms have been found to either reflect or increase pre-existing biases against certain groups of people.

We must remember that we are Christians. We have a call to justice. We also have a call to love our neighbours as ourselves. Because we have those obligations, we must stay alert to the ways in which AI can come to be used in ways that harm others or perpetuate patterns of inequality. Central to that, too, is to be advocating for AI that is ethical. For a way of developing and deploying those technologies that respects our values of fairness, respect and dignity for all people.

AI and Human Identity

And then there's the question of what it means to be human. As AI becomes more capable of ecosystems of human consciousness, we're exploring just how easily these systems can mimic humankind, from conversational exchange to creativity. This sort of behavioural mimicry tends to complicate the topic of human nature, of humanity and our unique place in God's creation.

However, as Christians, we believe that we are made not just in the mind of God, or with the mind of God, but are indeed made in the image of God (Imago Dei), that which makes us different from all other theological creations. No matter how efficient or accurate it may be, AI will never be capable of replicating the divine spark that makes us worthy and that gives us the capacity to relate to God and to make moral decisions. Maintaining this distinction is an important task in a world where AI is likely to forget.

Conclusion: Embracing AI with Discernment

Learning how to learn AI isn't just learning how AI works; it's learning how it relates to our Christian faith and values, testing together what wisdom and discernment do as we're encountering AI, learning to use it wisely, learning how it might serve the light and life and holiness and truth of the Gospel and the body of Christ, and learning how to guard against how it could lead us into the ways of the darkness and become an instrument of death and lies. Learning to pray through AI – learning Scripture through AI – can shape our engagement with it in a way that will help us use it wisely to empower God's kingdom and all whom he has made to come alive in him and flourish.

Remember once more, as you read this book, that AI is just a tool. A tool is no better nor worse than the people who use it. Armed with appropriate regulation and thoughtful, Christ-centred engagement, we can use AI to help us grow spiritually, build up communities, and minister to others in the love and imitation of our Lord and Saviour, Jesus Christ.

CHAPTER THREE

AI and the Bible: Discerning Wisdom in a Digital Age

As technology itself evolves rapidly, Christians must carefully consider how best to: develop a Christian approach to such tools; use them wisely; and protect us from those who would misuse them. The Bible is the living and Ancient Word of God: it contains eternal wisdom to guide our steps in all aspects of our lives. Here we offer guidelines on engaging with artificial intelligences and answer important questions that will shape how we use AI in a biblical way.

AI as a Tool for Biblical Study

But for Christians, one of the most exciting potential applications of AI relates to how we study our sacred texts. We're already great at that, of course. But we're also pretty good at the occasional wearisome toil and drudgery. One of AI's great benefits lies in its ability to rapidly sift through mountains of data, none of which the human brain could ever hope to process in a single lifetime.

For instance, AI can help folks cross-reference biblical passages, put text into historical and cultural context, even interpret difficult text – explaining how a word or phrase might mean one thing in today's English, while something very different in its original context. One online resource for Bible readers allows AI to scan for the frequency and usage of any specific Greek or Hebrew word throughout the Bible. This can help readers grasp a word's semantic range in different contexts. AI can also help study Bibles create tailored Bible-study plans to fit each reader's spiritual needs and vocation.

But far from replacing study or the guidance of the Holy Spirit, these AI tools were intended to supplement them. They were wholly compatible with religious orthodoxy, and they could make it easier for believers to glean a richer, more nuanced understanding of God's Word – and access some resources they might have otherwise never learned about.

The Importance of Discernment

Christians need to take a critical approach to the way they use AI. As with all human-produced tech, these tools are only as good as the data that they spit out. This means that AI-generated interpretations of Scripture or anything else are as good as the data fed into those systems. In turn, that data will reflect whatever bias or inadequacies humans bring to the problem.

After Christian readers are guided by our overarching principle: the authority of Scripture as the Word of God. If we thought that Bible study insights derived from self-learning AI were God-given truth, we could fall prey to the sin of idolatry. Surely, AI in Bible study cannot become a new idol for human life. The question that provides the direction of our faith is: 'What does the Bible say?' And how does God's Spirit speak to us, especially through the beloved words of Scripture? Given that AI-generated Bible study insights are just that – the machine's output, not a new revelation from beyond, they must always be weighed against our over-arching principles.

Also, as content is personalised, new spiritual echo chambers may be created, where users believe that they are exploring new and provocative interpretations and teachings but are only exposed to readings and content that reinforce their own views. Too much personalisation of study plans can not only be unhelpful ('How many times do I really need to read the character study on Job?') but can also hinder a person's faith from being stretching or challenging. Just because I never encounter anyone's perspective other than my own, does not mean I've grown in my faith, even though an AI would consider it statistically and algorithmically to have done so. The use of AI as a search tool can be mitigated by reading in a broad and eclectic fashion, and it's a good idea to make sure one maintains a healthy set of journals, encyclopaedias and learning resources that the Holy Spirit might lead you to.

AI and Biblical Interpretation: A Double-Edged Sword

Among these more difficult questions is speech 2: what role can AI play in biblical interpretation? More than authenticated sermons or easier searches for church history information, this is an area where unnecessary 'help' could be humiliating at best and spiritually damaging at worst. Laypeople often come to clergy with rote questions about Bible verses expressed as commandments: 'Does this mean I should make a vow to God if he helps me pass the big test at work?' Well-intentioned Christian writers have routinely treated the Bible in this manner over the centuries (God as cosmic genie) while leaving the underlying metaphors unrefined. What does it mean to 'vow' to God in a culture of specific oaths to uphold or to give to? Or what does 'song' mean to a 21st-century reader when it was a form of costing to have a band 'compose' an ode to a goddess' wedding? The upshot is that black-letter biblical passages never tell us about the sufficient context for their reading. They're always just a starting point for due consideration, prayer and wisdom from the community of faith. This is the role that theologians, pastors and scholars have primarily been called upon to play in biblical interpretation. But an AI can process and examine biblical texts at a level of scale, power and speed far beyond humans.

There are pros and cons to this capacity. It's a positive thing that AI can detect patterns in Scripture that human readers would miss, offering new avenues of enquiry. AI can cross-reference themes between biblical books; provide similar passages; and, using linguistic and historical data, might even have some things to say about what they mean.

Yet, there is an important question in using AI to divine and discern meaning from Scripture. AI itself cannot yet discern these spiritual or moral dimensions. It cannot pray nor can it be filled with the Holy Spirit and reason like the Holy Spirit is said to do. It cannot place biblical verses into the larger context of what the Christian faith teaches. Therefore, no matter how insightful the analyses might be, AI cannot replace the holy reading that a person of faith must do while prayerfully studying God's written word with divinely inspired insight.

But if Christians worry that AI-generated interpretations will mislead them, don't blame the technology. Blame your catechism. Let it help you to catch up to speed, then deepen your understanding and prayer. Christians should rightly fear the temptations of technological determinism. But we should condemn technological over-reliance more. Our technology-infused society measures the advancement of civilisation by its technical progress. The youth of today are told they can have any life they desire, but they can't because we haven't developed the technologies and AI interpretations necessary to get us there. We instinctively believe that a future full of technology – animated films, talking robots, immersive video-game realities, handheld smartphones that could transform us – would bring about a better age. The problem isn't technological substance, it's over-reliance. Christians should rightly fear the temptations of technological determinism. But we should condemn technological over-reliance more. We should be suspicious of any technology that relaxes our already lax religious sensibilities – especially if it mythologises, demythologises, secularises, or humanises God Himself. With that in mind, Christians need not fear the abilities of AI to 'save us from ourselves'. Rather, we must be wary of placing our trust in their ability to interpret Scripture for us – not as an end, but rather as a starting point for study and prayer.

Engaging with Scripture in the Digital Age

The present era is witnessing, if anything, the Bible as a hypertextual object, with myriad editions and commentaries, if not also the most recent translations, at the ready with just a few keystrokes. It is not difficult to imagine that AI-infused platforms and artificial intelligence can further advance this hyper accessibility to the study of Scripture, bringing us unprecedented opportunities to engage in informed and enlightening Bible study.

But access alone is insufficient unless it becomes accompanied by intention. It's all too easy to slip into skimming the canon for friendly soundbites or to become resigned to having all the Bible's wisdom summarised for us by generative AI. If the Bible is to form us, as it has formed believers for millennia, we must both approach and read it with the kind of attentiveness and reverence expected of those who live by its words.

We should use it with a discerning heart, always allowing Scripture, not AI, to be our authority. We should be mindful of AI's limitations, seek the help of the Holy Spirit, and study within a prayerful and communal context.

To conclude: there are seemingly unlimited possibilities for AI to enhance biblical scholarship, and great potential for growth in our knowledge of God's word and for living that word out in a digital age. However, there are many ways to use AI that should be avoided. We can only say that to use tools of AI as assistants and aids to study – and check our own discernment – can lead to a better understanding of God's revelation of himself.

CHAPTER FOUR

Prayer and AI: Enhancing Your Spiritual Communication

Prayer can be the most personal, private dimension of our life in God as Christians. It involves conversing with God and entrusting our hearts to Christ, discussing and discerning with the Spirit, and interceding on behalf of others. So, it should be unnerving to imagine Artificial Intelligence being somehow present in our prayer life. Perhaps even, something only spiritually immature people would think of. But AI can play a helpful part in spiritual communication that's meaningful and reflects God's character – if we do so in the right way.

AI as a Support Tool for Prayer

At its best, AI becomes an ancillary aid that empowers, rather than takes the place of, our prayer life. Perhaps the most obvious place that AI can help in prayer is by helping us to remember and keep track of it. We live such fragmented lives that it is easy to forget to prayer. AI-enabled alerts can remind us, keeping prayer on our radar throughout the day.

Beyond prompts, AI can assist in the structure of prayer by providing guided prayer sessions that offer scriptures, prompts and reflective questions to help organise prayer time for those who may struggle with what to pray for, or how to stay focused. This type of AI tool aims to aid in developing a more consistent and steady prayer habit.

One example is prayer journaling. Christians often find it useful to keep a journal of their prayers and of how God has answered or been involved in their lives over time. Apps powered by AI can be helpful with this by keeping track of entries and their themes, or suggesting scriptures or prayers related to the content of a given entry. Through such apps, we could not only keep track of how we are walking with God, but also see what kinds of challenges or praises keep reoccurring in our lives as we pray each month or year.

AI and Prayer: Potential Pitfalls

It's not to say that AI can't be used beneficially and help us in our walk with God, but we need to be aware of the dangers as well. For example, presumably, prayer is a very personal thing, an intimate dialogue with God informed by our relationship with him. If we end up using AI-generated prompts or tools in our prayer lives, there is a danger that our prayers could become rote, or worse, mechanical.

Also, AI can't provide that intimate discernment of the spiritual and emotional dimensions of our lives that only another human being can. Yes, AI might be able to give us helpful prompts about when and how to pray, but it can't divine our hearts' deep needs or be tuned into the guidance of the Holy Spirit. In other words, AI can support our prayer life, but it is no substitute for speaking directly to our Creator from the depths of our own hearts.

A second concern might be privacy. Prayer is frequently private. When we pray, we engage in private speech, so using AI technologies to pray raises certain concerns. At a minimum, it means having some awareness of what data is being collected and how it is being used. These issues are mitigated by the variety of AI prayer tools that include strict privacy limits.

AI as a Tool for Intercessory Prayer

Praying on behalf of others (known as intercessory prayer) is also a significant feature of the Christian life, and AI could be immensely helpful in this arena, for example by helping us to organise and remember the needs of those for whom we pray. AI-assisted prayer lists could group requests into categories, schedule reminders for follow-up, and give quick access to relevant scriptures or readymade prayers. Church communities or house groups often receive lots of prayer requests, for example, and these might overlap or build on each other.

Beyond that, AI can enable global intercession by linking people with prayer needs from around the globe. Some apps and platforms use AI to pool prayer requests from around the world, enabling Christians to pray for things and people that they might well have been unaware of. A global outlook can expand our sense of the Body of Christ – it can provide a window for expanding prayer lives.

Enhancing Your Spiritual Communication with AI

Remember that AI is a tool and always think of it that way: it should complement, not replace, a meaningful interaction and intimate dialogue with God. Here's how to integrate AI into prayer:

1. Set Healthy Boundaries: Use the AI for your reminders and structure, but make sure the core of your prayer time is still a one-on-one conversation with God. Do not let it become too reliant on AI-generated prompts and scripting. Instead, use them as starting points for deeper reflection.

2. Keep it Private: Avoid open or sharing apps and seek out an AI tool that allows you to manage your prayer data in a way that integrates with your personal privacy. you don't have to share your prayers with a digital platform unless you want to. There are plenty of tools and apps that allow you to keep your practice offline or anonymous.

3. Shaping Guidance into Spontaneity: Use the guidance, prompts, prompts and prayer-makers of AI-assisted prayer but leave extra space for spontaneity, where your prayer time is influenced by the Holy Spirit and the AI becomes some sort of support for how God might lead your time of intercession and communion.

4. Live in Community: Use AI to make intercessory prayer efficient and coordinated, not only for your personal prayer list but for the needs of your community, too. But allow prayer to also be more communal; prayer isn't just a private exercise of the soul – it's communal. Think about the communal elements of praying together at church, in small groups or in large crowds, for instance. AI can assist and complement this dimension of prayer (as in any aspect of the Christian life) but should not replace it.

5. Periodically Check-in on How AI is Affecting Your Practice: This seems like a good time to assess where your use of AI is taking your prayer life, and whether this is affirming your experience of connecting with God, or whether the very use of AI is distracting you from your practice. Adjust your use of AI accordingly.

Conclusion: Embracing AI with Prayerful Intent

Prayer is a deeply personal interaction with God and AI has great potential to support that experience by increasing the effectiveness of our prayer life, helping us organise and remember our prayer times, keeping us on track and making prayer a more global experience. But all good technology, no matter how profound, should be used discerningly, so that it is a tool supporting our spiritual communication, and not a tool that diminishes the personal and divine aspect of prayer.

In the right spirit of prayer, and if we integrate AI well into our lives, technology can lead us into a closer relationship to God, to remain mindful of the needs of others, and to a more meaningful prayer-life. May we welcome AI as a servant, not to replace the Holy Spirit, but to lead us closer to the God who hears all that we say.

CHAPTER FIVE

Devotional Life in the Digital Age: Tools for Daily Inspiration

So many things in a Christian's daily life are marked by rhythm: regular meals, regular work schedules, regular holidays, and (at least in the predigital era) regular bedtimes. Daily devotional practices — prayer, readings, and study — can also be rhythmed, and this gives a consistent element to our spiritual practice. Of course, these are not the kind of rhythms that make your body sway; they are not that predictable. Nonetheless, each prayer has its place in the shape of your day, and your trajectory through a psalm becomes a way maker for your own inner life. Your devotional practice is a discipline designed to help you learn to return to God inside and outside the regular milestones of your day. The addition of digital technology raises new questions and enables novel practices. We need to be both careful and creative to employ our digital technology in the service of a deeper devotional life. In this chapter, I explore how AI-driven tools can augment your 'devotional habit' and offer some tips on how to use them well.

The Role of Devotionals in a Christian's Life

These experiences, often known as devotionals, intentionally give Christians a set time each day to focus on God's Word and on growing in their love and obedience to him. Whether this involves reading or meditating on a portion of Scripture, reflecting on a particular spiritual truth, or praying through a thoughtful idea, the importance of regularly engaging in devotionals is difficult to overstate. Among the many blessings these brief episodes of attention bring is the opportunity they provide to take our chaotic lives and centre them upon Christ.

Devotionals were once done with a printed Bible, a devotional book, maybe a journal for taking notes and reflections. These tools still have their place, but digital tools promise to add to the practical resources of this ancient worship practice. AI takes personalised devotion what has previously been available only to a select few.

AI-Powered Devotional Tools

AI could assist you enormously in devotional life, through daily content tailored to where you are in your spiritual journey Many pocket-based AI-powered apps or platforms now offer daily devotionals, which they tailor to your specific needs, interests and spiritual goals. They will, for example, suggest Bible passages relevant to the themes you're focusing on in your life; recommend specific prayers based on your life context; or make suggestions about reflections that will challenge you in ways you need to be challenged.

One of the most helpful features of the AI-powered devotionals is that they get to know you better and can adapt and change along with your needs. The more you use the tools consistently, the more they learn about what you truly like to read, how you respond, and how you like to digest verbiage. That should make your devotional time more effective and relevant.

Also, there are AI tools and apps that can assist you to remain focused in your devotion. For instance, there are apps that send prayer reminders/notifications to encourage you to set time for prayer. Some of them even track your streak and progress, which will potentially impel you to maintain your regular devotion.

Integrating Digital Devotionals into Your Routine

Although AI-powered devotionals have much to offer us, it is important to assimilate them into our ritual observances in a way that adds to rather than detracts from our spirituality. So, here are some practical suggestions for how to do that:

1. Clarify intentions: Before using a new digital devotional aid, pause to clarify intentions. What do you want to get out of your devotional regimen? How will the tool help to achieve those goals? Whether your goals include a deepening knowledge of the Bible, consistent prayer habits, or simply a moment of peace each morning, taking time to formulate your intentions will better equip you to use the aid.

2. Pick an App That Fits: There's no shortage of AI-powered devotional tools out there, so it's worth spending some time finding one that suits you and your spiritual needs and values. Look for a tool that's committed to both scriptural accuracy and to making theologically sound observations and reflections and respects your privacy. Reviews and recommendations from other Christians can also be useful.

3. Mark a Sacred Space: Cultivate a space, even when using digital tools, perhaps a special chair or corner of your home or a certain park bench, that is reserved for your devotion time, that can guide your wandering mind to reverence for the Lord.

4. AI Powered Tools: Let's face it, I will keep writing and publishing biblical studies with the help of AI-powered tools. But so should I also get my own hands dirty dusting off my well-worn physical Bible and take some time to reflect on God's Word by writing down my reflections in an old-school journal. Or maybe I'll even set aside some time for intentional, purposeful, spiritual silence – even if the initial experience of it prompts words such as, 'What in the world was I thinking?' Maybe your situation is different. In any case, all of us who seek to constantly erode barriers that arise between our lives of faith – such as setting aside periods of intentional digital abstinence so that you can more readily receive the grace God has provided in the world outside the confines of digital fog – alongside your utilisation of cutting-edge artificial intelligence.

5. Avoid Distractions: One of the possible pitfalls of using digital tools to meet with God are distractions. Digitally delivered notifications, messages and other forms of digital distractions can affect your devotional time. You might combat this issue by selecting apps that have an option for 'do not disturb' during your devotional time or placing your device on airplane mode.

The Potential Drawbacks of Digital Devotionals

Ultimately, while AI-based devotionals can be helpful, we should be mindful of the pitfalls. The first is the risk of technological complacency; these tools can and should complement your devotional life, not replace it. The core of your devotional life is your direct, personal communion with God through prayer and Scripture reading.

Another problem could be consumerism. You might inadvertently sign up for a devotional app, or follow a devotional minute's feed, where the commodifiable is more important than the beneficial, the entertaining than the edifying. Quality and purpose need to be discerned. Ask yourself if what you see supports truth from God's Word.

Moreover, AI's particularisation also risks creating what we might call devotional echo chambers, in which you're offered more from the same topic or theme simply because you've engaged with it recently or through a specific pathway. Content that resonates with you can help you reflect on that, and it can act as a form of spiritual protection and care. But we can also risk getting too close to our lives if the repetition means that we're not encountering anything new. This can be addressed by securing a balanced spiritual diet, including the reading or listening to analogue, 'stationary' devotional materials.

Conclusion: Embracing AI as a Tool for Growth

It's possible that AI might make your devotional life richer by offering customised content or reminders or tools in a way that helps you maintain your morning (or evening) with God in a way that has never been so possible before; yet it is also possible that these tools will be too invasive – nudging you into a subpar spiritual life that would have been better off avoided in favour of your own prayer, scripture reading, study or meditation. The point is that new tools are coming your way soon that might enrich your on-the-go devotional life – but no matter what they are or how they are intended to be used, it's up to you to wrestle over whether you want to adopt them or not. You get to decide what kind of devotional life you want.

Used thoughtfully, you can enhance your devotional life as you help it become more consistent, relevant to your day and your walk with the Lord. These tools are exactly that: tools to assist you in your walk with the Lord. The quality of your devotional life will not come about because of your technology but rather because of the faithfulness of your relationship with the Lord.

CHAPTER SIX

AI-Driven Bible Study: Deepening Your Scriptural Knowledge

Scripture is the cornerstone on which the Christian life is built. The Bible reveals the nature and the will of God, and it teaches the law of God, by means of which human beings understand and comply with what they are called to be and to do. While studying Scripture has long been one of the most fundamental ways that Christian believers pursue a living connection with and awareness of God, the constraints of traditional ways of studying have restricted its value for many in the Church. By leveraging the power of AI, it becomes possible to AI tools, your Bible study becomes more interactive and opens your eyes to a truly Christian experience.

The Evolution of Bible Study Tools

The study of the Bible has always been in some sense a scholarly discipline; serious study has always entailed making use of one or more commentaries on the text, a lexicon of New Testament Greek words and expressions, and a concordance (a reference book documenting where the various words are used) to gain a better grasp of the meaning of the text. Such study often takes time (sometimes a lot of it) but it is also richly rewarding – as long as you have access to the necessary library of resources.

In the digital age, Bible study has been both democratised and accelerated. Online resources and mobile applications grant ready-to-assemble access to multiple translations, commentaries and study guides in a single session. AI accelerates biblical study further, making suggestions and connections that manual study might miss or overlook.

How AI Enhances Bible Study

AI-driven Bible study tools can enhance your understanding of Scripture in several ways:

1.**Cross-Referencing and Thematic Analysis:** One of the most powerful features of AI is its ability to cross-reference passages and identify themes across the entire Bible. For example, if you're studying a particular topic like forgiveness, an AI tool can quickly pull together relevant verses from both the Old and New Testaments, offering a comprehensive view of the biblical teaching on the subject.

2. **Original Language Insights:** Understanding the original languages of the Bible—Hebrew, Aramaic, and Greek—can significantly deepen your understanding of the text. AI-driven tools can analyse the original language, providing insights into the meanings of words and phrases that are not always apparent in translation. This allows for a more nuanced interpretation of Scripture.

3. **Contextual Understanding:** AI tools can provide historical and cultural context for the passages you're studying. By integrating data from

archaeological findings, historical documents, and other sources, these tools can help you understand the world in which the Bible was written, offering a richer and more informed reading of the text.

4. Personalized Study Plans: AI can create personalized Bible study plans based on your spiritual needs, interests, and schedule. Whether you want to study a specific book of the Bible, explore a particular theme, or follow a daily reading plan, AI can tailor a study program that fits your goals and helps you stay on track.

5. Interactive Learning: Many AI-driven tools offer interactive features, such as quizzes, discussion questions, and multimedia content, to engage you in a more dynamic study experience. These features can help reinforce your learning and make Bible study more engaging and enjoyable.

The Benefits of AI-Driven Bible Study

AI-driven Bible study tools offer several benefits that can enhance your spiritual growth:

1. Efficiency: AI can save you time by quickly pulling together resources, cross-references, and insights that would take hours to gather manually. This efficiency allows you to spend more time reflecting on the text and applying it to your life.

2. Depth: By providing access to original language tools, historical context, and thematic analysis, AI can help you gain a deeper understanding of Scripture. This depth of study can lead to greater spiritual insight and a more profound relationship with God.

3. Accessibility: AI-driven tools make advanced Bible study resources accessible to everyone, regardless of their level of theological training. Whether you're a new believer or a seasoned scholar, these tools can help you explore the Bible in new and meaningful ways.

4. Consistency: Personalized study plans and reminders can help you maintain a consistent Bible study routine, ensuring that you stay engaged with Scripture even during a busy life.

Challenges and Considerations

While AI-driven Bible study tools offer many advantages, it's important to approach them with discernment. Here are some challenges and considerations to keep in mind:

1. Over-Reliance on Technology: While AI can enhance your Bible study, it's important not to become overly reliant on technology. The Holy Spirit plays a vital role in guiding your understanding of Scripture, and this spiritual discernment should always take precedence over AI-generated insights.

2. Theological Biases: AI tools are created by humans, and as such, they can reflect the theological biases of their developers. It's important to be aware of these biases and to critically evaluate the insights provided by AI tools, always comparing them against the truth of Scripture.

3. Privacy Concerns: As with any digital tool, privacy is a consideration. Be mindful of the data you share and the potential for your study habits to be tracked or analysed. Choose tools that prioritize user privacy and offer secure options for managing your data.

4. Superficial Engagement: The convenience of AI-driven tools can sometimes lead to a more superficial engagement with Scripture. It's important to balance the efficiency of AI with deep, reflective study and prayer, ensuring that your Bible study remains a meaningful and transformative practice.

Conclusion: AI as a Partner in Spiritual Growth

AI-driven Bible study tools offer exciting opportunities to deepen your knowledge of Scripture and grow in your faith. By providing personalized, efficient, and in-depth resources, these tools can make Bible study more accessible and engaging for believers at all levels.

However, it's crucial to use these tools as partners in your spiritual growth, not as replacements for the personal, prayerful study that is essential to a vibrant faith. By approaching AI-driven Bible study with discernment and intentionality, you can harness the power of technology to enrich your understanding of God's Word and draw closer to Him in your daily walk.

CHAPTER SEVEN

Building a Virtual Christian Community: Connecting in Christ Online

A s our world converses more and more through Twitter and FB, as our virtual spaces collide with physical spaces to re-create our reality, it calls us Christians to think deeply about how to utilise our tools in perfecting and reconciling our online environments to promote authentic Christian community. What are these opportunities and challenges, and how can we make sense of this landscape? At first glance, many people would say that AI has no place in building community authentically. Humans should be the priority. However, I don't think this is entirely true. First, I think humans can benefit from the use of AI in community. Second, AI seems to be going to great lengths to complement and mimic human interactions. Community is now the epicentre of evangelism, gathering, and humanising life. I believe Christians could use their toolset, especially AI, to build and nurture authentic Christian community online. This chapter will explore some of these tools. To ensure that your Christian community becomes a faithful representation of Christ, here are some helpful steps to leveraging AI for your new or expanded community online.

The Rise of Virtual Communities

However, since the establishment of the internet and the spread of social media worldwide, spaces for this type of togetherness expanded greatly. Such virtual communities are social units that exist mainly through digital media and communication technologies. To this end, for Christians, these online spaces have provided a way to stay together, even when the actual bodily aggregation is not possible: from social media groups to virtual Bible studies, until online services, the use of technology has made possible new ways of being together beyond the confines of time and space.

But virtual communities also bring their own problems. Interaction online can feel sterile and cold, in contrast with real-time, face-to-face gatherings that provide a more organic forum for getting to know others. The sheer mass of available information and opportunities to interact can be an impediment to forming deep, ongoing connections.

How AI Can Enhance Virtual Christian Communities

If we are willing to make the effort, AI could possibly play a major role in strengthening online Christian communities. Here are five ways that this might happen.

1.Personalised Content/Engagement: AI can help being to understand the individual preferences, interests and spiritual needs of individuals living in a community using sentiment and speech detection capabilities and responds by providing targeted content such as Bible verses, devotionals or topic prompts to match individuals' needs at the time.

2. Small Groups: Helping people navigate and pray for each other small groups are at the heart of many congregations. AI can help facilitate these through matching people with others who have the same interests, spiritual maturity or life stage. It could provide discussion topics, study resources and can track prayer requests or follow-up conversations to help people feel known and remembered.

3. Moderation and Stewardship: Large online communities can have lively but difficult-to-control discussion forums. Moderation tools that use AI can be applied to promote respectful interactions, keep things grounded in a Christ-centred perspective, and mark conversations or submissions that are positive and well suited in this environment.

4. Improving Access: In the physical world, the need for AI to be 'human' diminishes, and our new perspective allows us to look back to the physical world and help our avatars benefit from it. AI can offer us services such as live translation for non-native speakers, speech-to-text for those who prefer to read rather than listen, or customised forms of content for those who learn better visually or by listening. This means that everyone with special needs can have access to an environment that allows them to participate as peers on an equal level.

5. Spiritual Care: AI systems could assist with tracking spiritual growth – by sending out daily reflections, keeping you up to date on your prayer journal, helping you expand your Scripture memory, and offering encouragement along the way. It could boost member commitment by keeping them on track with their spiritual disciplines.

Challenges of Building Virtual Christian Communities with AI

Even though AI has its benefits, developing Christian virtual communities must also contend with some dangers and disadvantages accumulated along the way.

1. Superficial Connections: The primary risk of virtual communities is that our connections with people will stay superficial – that technology might increase engagement, but not the meaningful face-to-face interactions of real life. We need to figure out how to move beyond the surface more often, possibly planning virtual community meetups in person, or simply encouraging smaller groups of people to connect.

2. Privacy and security: Managing online communities with AI means collecting and analysing data, and hence privacy and security issues are important in this context. Practices and actions of online community leaders must protect community member privacy, and people must be informed about how their data is used.

3. Centering in Christ: One issue for any community is trust. Who can we trust? Artificial intelligence can be a great new tool, but it should never become the centre of the story – Scripture, prayer and the indwelling of the Holy Spirit must always remain at the centre. Community leaders must keep a watchful eye to ensure that AI is used as a tool for these things, rather than a replacement for them.

4. How to handle digital distractions: Internet communities are swamped with content that can draw members away from important interactions. AI can help with editorial control, but so can cultivating a culture in which members take responsibility for their time and give full attention during their interactions.

Best Practices for Creating a Thriving Virtual Christian Community

To build and sustain a thriving virtual Christian community, consider the following best practices:

1. Cultivate Genuine Relationships: Inspire members to live transparently and with integrity. Let AI foster 'free-flow conversations' but also offer space for members to bear their souls more directly, in prayer partnerships, or in small groups.

2 Prioritise discipleship: Keep the church's culture focused on forming disciples. Use AI to enable this goal by curating resources that enable growth, tracking development, suggesting readings and assignments, and providing encouragement and coaching.

3. Define group membership: Help every member feel seen and heard AI can create personalised content and engagement flows but there is no replacement for personal relationships and direct care. For example, leaders can make their accessibility known, calling or visiting people who may be new to the group, less engaged, or simply feeling isolated.

4. Build Accountability: Encourage members to hold one another accountable within their respective spiritual lives.AI plays role, through tracking commitments and prompting remembering of one's own goals, but personal accountability requires people as well.

5. Stay fluid and open: Stay receptive to feedback and open to making changes to the structure of the community and the methods members employ as situations arise. Use AI to inform, but not substitute, individual and collective decisions inspired by the Holy Spirit and the needs of the community.

Conclusion: Embracing AI in Building Christ-Centered Connections

AI could open indirect channels for building and enhancing virtual Christian communities, lending each believer the support, growth, and edification they desire, tie us to the Body of Christ and sustain us, not just in our everyday communal life, but in our journey toward salvation, when we've crossed into the twilight zone and can't depend on the usual systems and structures any longer. Such endeavours can succeed, yet in a way that enables us flourish through prayer, if we're thoughtful and deliberate in utilising AI for these purposes – always remaining oriented to the face of Christ.

By committing to authentic relationships, focusing on discipleship, and anointing our communities with the spirit of Christ, we can find ourselves inhabiting virtual communities that not only endure in the new digital epoch but also embrace it. Just like our face-to-face communities of faith, virtual communities can become centres of grace, encouragement and discipleship. They can aid us in walking with Christ – wherever we might live in this brave new world.

CHAPTER EIGHT

AI for Ministry: Serving Others with Tech Innovations

Ministry is at the centre of Christian proclamation and the basis for Christian hope. It is an expression of God's love for the world that Christians are called to emulate as we help others. As we seek to fulfil that calling, Christians are using technological advances to aid their ministries. What about AI? Can AI – artificial intelligence – aid in Christian ministry? This chapter explores how AI can further ministries of pastoral care and other examples of Christian ministry to those in our communities. It concludes with a discussion of some of the questions of ethics that practitioners should consider as they reflect on whether AI is an appropriate technology to use in their ministry settings.

The Role of AI in Pastoral Care

A traditional role of pastoral care is to act as a spiritual guide, to provide support and to offer advice. It has long been an intimate ministry, often conducted face-to-face and involving prayer and the sharing of Scripture, so it wouldn't seem possible that artificial intelligence would be a useful addition for those engaging in this type of work, especially as their churches become larger and more widely spread.

1. Pastoral tools: For counselling, AI can build tools that help the pastor track and engage the various spiritual and emotional needs of the congregation. An AI-driven platform might analyse prayer requests and counselling notes to detect patterns that could indicate need or call for further action. Such tools could also recommend resources to help the person seeking prayer – perhaps relevant Bible verses, an article or a conference on the matter.

2. Virtual Pastoral: Timothy Shelley's Windows-based prayer bot 'PC Pastor', achievable with readily available artificial intelligence. Virtual Pastoral Assistant   expect to perform pastoral duties 24/7 to meet the needs of its members. What about technologies that encompass a 'virtual pastoral assistant' to serve as pastoral Godot for a churchgoer? A chatbot or virtual assistant who can answer a common question, provide a prayer, deliver a brief Scripture reading – or, for something a bit more ambitious, who can evaluate emotional needs and summarise the relevant pastoral comments stored in a library of resources? Of course, these tools will not and should not replace the human part of pastoral ministry. Picture pastors everywhere recoiling in horror at the idea of usurping pastoral ministry through the promise of a quick, easy fix. The experience of having a human shepherd represents something unique that we cannot fully develop with a computer-based program, however useful it might be to have one. And yet, even if it is not a replacement, for many pastors expect to perform pastoral duties 24/7 in order to meet the needs of its members. If a congregant calls or texts and asks a simple question after hours, it could provide an immediate answer.

3. Better Communication: Chaplain AI can help pastors better communicate on their church's behalf by analysing engagement data, and tailoring messages to various members or groups. It may be able to identify members who are less engaged or struggling with their faith, for example, to deliver specialised notes of encouragement and support.

AI in Community Outreach

Community outreach, a crucial part of Christian ministry, can be served by tailoring the gospel outside the walls of the church. AI can support these efforts by helping churches identify needs, organising resources, and engaging more efficiently with their various communities.

1.Concerning community needs: An AI, combing through social media feeds, local news reporting, and government statistics, could tabulate pressing needs in the neighbourhood. Maybe people need food assistance, or shelter. Perhaps many are suffering from mental illness. Understanding these needs helps churches figure out how to address them.

2. Volunteer and Resource-Coordination: AI can be used to bring volunteers and resources together for community outreach projects. An AI-powered platform may be used to match volunteers to projects based on their appropriate skills, track availability of supplies, and optimise transport and planning for projects such as food drives or health clinics. This ensures that limited resources are mobilised efficiently and effectively.

3. Community Outreach: AI can assist churches to reach out to the wider community by analysing information on social media trends and online engagement with the community and using this information to construct effective outreach campaigns and inviting community members to gatherings.

Weekly announcements at church meetings, dissemination of faith-based materials to members, or posting messages of hope and support for members of the community than those who don't.

Ethical Considerations in AI-Driven Ministry

If used rightly, AI could be a great boon to ministry. But right along with those positive best-case scenarios come serious ethical concerns that we all need to think through carefully as Christians and, wherever possible, work to steer clear of. When it comes to our ministries, we must use AI in ways that do not dehumanise Christ's Church or our fellow humans. The goal should always be to keep our technology serving our proper ends, not vice versa.

1. Ensuring human relationship: The risk that AI could replace human relationship is one of the biggest barriers for integrating AI into ministry today. Ministry is inherently relational. Pastoral ministry, counselling ministry and even ministries staffed by volunteers require the individual attention of a human being. AI support in ministry must supplement face-to-face human interactions that are standard in all types of Christian ministry today. It cannot replace it. Churches characterised by connection value the AI tool only as adjunct to not instead of personal ministry.

2. Ensuring Privacy and Confidentiality: Ministry often involves privacy, confidentiality and safeguarding sensitive data. Whether it be relating to personal struggles or prayer requests or content of counselling sessions, the privacy concerns transcend that of a normal app and the AI-driven tools that might be used to gather and utilise such data must be imbued with such privacy and confidentiality protections. Additionally, these apps will need to be transparent with its users in terms of how it utilises data and safeguards their personal information.

3. Avoiding Technological Centralisation: Though AI offers new possibilities for making ministry more efficient, the productivity offered might lead to an over-dependence on technology. The ministry is not only about optimisation of efficiency, but it is also about presence, pastoral compassion, and allowing the Holy Spirit to guide one's activity. Church leaders should remain keenly aware of this balance and should also ensure that the efficiencies promoted through technology enhance the spiritual and relational aspects of the ministry.

4. Tackling Bias and Fairness: An AI system can sometimes reflect the biases of its developers or what it was trained on. The ministry should be especially sensitive to this because AI tools should promote fairness and justice. Church leaders must be alert to any biases they may find in any AI tools they purchase or use, so as not to inadvertently bring about inequality or injustice.

Best Practices for Integrating AI into Ministry

To effectively integrate AI into ministry, consider the following best practices:

1. Occupy yourself with a clear focus: Before you dabble in new AI tools, ask yourself and your team what the clear focus of your ministry is, and how it can aid these efforts. This will assist you in choosing the best tools and avoiding the pitfalls of new chimpanzees.

2. Engage with Neighbours and Community: Bring your congregation and community into the process of experimentation, questioning, piloting and feedback. Help them understand how the technology might be used in ministry, and what it could enhance. Seek their input, address their concerns, and involve them as much as possible in the testing and feedback loops. So, there are eight ways that ministers can navigate the implementation of these emerging technologies. No two congregations and clergy are exactly alike, nor will two emerging-technology situations be identical; therefore, there is no simple solution to summarise and advise equally well on all of these situations. Even our survey results are limited because they provide only a snapshot view of what clergy are doing and how they are considering these emerging technologies. As new, pending and potential technologies continue to proliferate, our positions and approaches to emerging technologies will constantly require re-evaluation. However, we can start from the positions and approaches that we already occupy and make connections from there.

3. Put Training and Support in Place: Train pastors, ministry leaders and volunteers in how to use AI tools properly. Equip them not only with a positive approach to using AI but also how to avoid unconsciously relying on the tool too much and too often. Encourage them to use the technology to complement their ministry, not to replace it.

4. Monitor and Evaluate: Establish regular indicators to measure the impact of AI. Surveying and listening to feedback from the ministry community involved can help monitor outcomes. Evaluate whether AI-induced approaches or processes are working as intended. Make internal adjustments when necessary. This is an evolving cycle of engagement, always accounting for the challenges and opportunities of AI.

Conclusion: Serving Others with Innovation and Compassion

AI could allow pastors to better serve their communities by offering more effective and efficient forms of ministry. Pastors could then deploy AI in ways that make their ministry more responsive to the actual needs of their communities. Pastors, assistants and communities could all benefit from AI-enabled ministry that enhances pastoral care, improves outreach and enables other forms of service. Used thoughtfully, AI could enhance the power of pastoral ministry and transform, in creative and constructive ways, the work we do.

But as we do this, we must ever be intentional with AI, grounded in our Christian theology and allowing the technology to augment, rather than replace, the personal, relational and spiritual dimensions of ministry. With wisdom and discernment, and in the spirit of being servants of others in the name of Christ, we now possess the possibility to use technology to care for others in distinct, positive ways.

CHAPTER NINE

Ethical AI: Navigating Moral Challenges as Christians

With increasing implementation of technology and artificial intelligence (AI) in daily life, Christians will increasingly come up against moral issues that offer unique challenges for moral formation, questions about right and wrong, justice and mercy, and how best to live as the people of God in a digital world. One of the reasons that artificial intelligence offers unique moral challenges and puzzles is that AI makes choices, shapes (or lends) social norms, and influences behaviour. The aim of this chapter is to show how Christians might approach or think through these concerns or ethical conundrums so that, in the place of automatons as God's image-bearers, our use and creation of AI serves the call of the Bible to our humanity, to create with loving care and intentionality; a call that Christ himself exemplified for all his followers.

Understanding the Ethical Implications of AI

This ability of AI to process data, learn from data, and act according to patterns and algorithms that it learns from the data can spell both opportunities and risks: if such systems are used to address complex problems, improve efficiencies and create new innovations with positive socioeconomic benefit, this can be good. However, left unregulated these systems can perpetuate biases, violate privacy rights, and even cause unintended harm.

For Christians, the low-hanging fruit of AI ethics arise from the things we hold most central to our beliefs: that human life has inherent worth, that we are called to love our neighbours and do justice. Who is Jesus in AI? How does our use of it affect humans and human communities, especially the poor, burned and broken?

AI and Human Dignity

Perhaps the most significant ethical concern in an AI context has to do with respecting human dignity – the idea that any and every individual is created in the image of God (or, in non-theological terms, that each human being is of inestimable worth and value). AI technologies and their deployment should be designed and executed to respect the dignity of persons, so that those affected are afforded justice, respect and mercy.

Still, AI systems can affect human dignity in negative ways, such as when humans are treated as objects, as mere statistics or data, as in AI-driven forms of surveillance to monitor and control people, for instance, or in automated decision-making, including in hiring, lending and so on, which can discriminate against certain groups. Christians must raise our voice against the unethical use of AI systems, a technology that must not undermine human dignity.

Justice and Fairness in AI

The concept of justice is fundamental to Scripture and is also at the heart of the ethical use of AI. The design and operation of AI systems should always centre on the idea of fairness, and not pass on the existing injustices of society. When AI is created and trained using data, it can itself embody bias against certain groups. We're now familiar with news stories highlighting such instances. For instance, face-detection software has higher error rates for images of people with darker skin tones compared with those with lighter skin.

As Christians, we should push for justice and the vulnerable, by being concerned about ways in which AI exacerbates or perpetuates inequalities. We should commend those who seek to develop transparent, accountable, and non-biased AI systems. Moreover, we should work to increase exposure of AI harms and advocate for policies and practices that promote fairness and equity.

Privacy and Autonomy

Another pressing ethical issue related to AI is that of privacy. For many AI systems to function well, they need to be trained using large amounts of data. Sometimes this data is personal, and while AI can offer important benefits – for instance, improved healthcare – it is important to ensure that users give consent on how the data will be used, stored and collected.

Christians should advocate for the same rights of personal autonomy and informed choice about our individual lives today as we do tomorrow where these rights conflict with excessive state surveillance, infringements of privacy and unnecessary government authority, such as access to personal travel patterns tracked via AI systems today. Stricter regulations governing the amassing and use of personal data are needed, so that every input must be explained to each consumer before it can be used for any purpose, and there is a guarantee of anonymity. Ethical parameters are essential to regulate future systems, and strong data-protection laws need to continue to be in place.

AI and the Sanctity of Life

The second is the sacredness of life. This is part of the essence of the Christian faith. As technologies such as artificial intelligence (AI) evolve, particularly as AI can be directly connected to saving, sustaining and protecting it, we must reckon with more profound moral questions and challenges about how that technology is wielded. AI drives more and more medical diagnoses and treatment planning, as well as end-of-life care decisions.

If AI has the potential to improve outcomes and prolong life, we also need to be cognisant about its contributing to a utilitarian ethic that could devalue human life. Meaningful decisions about life and death belong to human beings, not machines, or even algorithms, and never without human judgment, compassion and ethical clarity. So, as Christians, we need to continue to advocate for the responsible design and integration of AI into healthcare. Our faith provides that through it, we will find meaning and purpose in this life, and when on this mortal soil we receive the hope of something eternal.

Ethical AI in the Workplace

AI is not just changing jobs, it's changing how work gets done, from automating rote tasks to optimising decision-making. While AI-enabled innovations can enhance workers' productivity, it is also possible that they adversely affect employment by displacing workers or rendering their labour obsolete. The advent of AI has the potential to shift labour markets, thereby resulting in job losses or changes to the nature of work.

So, Christians should use our power of influence – through our votes, our advocacy, our buying power and so much more – to push for worker-friendly policies. As Christians, we should also consider how AI and other technologies could make workplaces more just and equitable, whether through better monitoring to prevent sexual harassment or the exploitation of workers.

Best Practices for Ethical AI

To navigate the ethical challenges of AI, Christians can adopt several best practices:

1. Prayer for Wisdom and Discernment: Pray that God will give you wisdom and discernment about how you use or interact with AI. Pray that God will direct your path and show you His will for your life.

2. Learn and Educate: Keep up with AI ethics and educate others around you. Learn about AI ethics risks and benefits and help others become more aware.

3. Push for Ethical Guidelines: Promote the development and spread of ethical guidelines for AI. This allows people to push for key principles around transparency, accountability and fairness in AI.

4. Human-Centred AI: Facilitate the proliferation of AI technologies that incorporate human dignity, equality and justice, for instance by sponsoring programmes countering bias or abusive actions, strengthening privacy protections or ensuring the sacredness of life.

5. Make Ethical Decisions: Now that you have an AI component, how do you use it ethically in your own life or as a part of your job? Think about how your actions affect others and how you can promote the greater good of all.

Conclusion: Upholding Christian Values in a Digital World

Christians, for their part, have a chance to demonstrate their thoughtfulness and faithfulness in responding prophetically and pastorally to the new challenges emerging in a world increasingly shaped by the rise of AI. In the wake of this technological ascendancy, animations like Toy Story could do a lot worse than seek guidance from the wisdom presented in God's revelation to his people, the Bible.

In doing so, we can bear witness in a digital world, showing that technology can be used for good and bringing glory to God in all that we do.

CHAPTER TEN

Parenting in a High-Tech World: Guiding the Next Generation with Faith

Navigating childhood in the high-tech world of the 21st century calls for discernment, spiritual wisdom and a vision for the spiritual health of our kids. After all, 21st century parents must shepherd the emergence of our children's humanity in the ever-shifting sands of Artificial Intelligence (AI). The ways kids learn and interact are increasingly influenced by AI, a game-changing reality that Christian parents will need to consider raising thoughtful and strong children of faith. This chapter offers concrete recommendations for the courageous and adventurous task of raising God-formed human beings in a rapidly changing world of technological transformation.

Understanding the Influence of AI on Childhood

Today's children represent a digital generation that has been born into a world of smart toys and devices, and the widespread use and acceptance of AI technologies that enable and inform daily life. From providing entertainment to facilitating education, a large variety of AI technologies have been tailored to engage, delight and inform. Such tools may assist children in acquiring skills and knowledge, and even in reading and math. Given proper guidance, programming and context, personalised learning apps for educational purposes represent a perfect use for AI. When well-implemented, children learn in a safe and isolated environment that provides real-time feedback, allowing for the platform to adapt to a child's learning style and pace.

Yet at the same time the very pervasiveness of AI brings some risks: algorithms can mediate children's information landscape, for example, and they don't always curate digital content in ways that optimise learning value, with commercial aims often guiding the algorithms. Prolonged engagement in mediated digital reality can result in too much screentime, harmful for various reasons – it can diminish attention, harm sleep, and interfere with the development of social skills. Christian parents face opportunities as well as challenges in this mediated world. They must be more discerning in how they steer and encourage their children in their usage of AI, for human beings were made for real relationships and real experiences, not digital substitutes for them.

Setting Healthy Boundaries for Technology Use

Setting clear, healthy limits around technology use is one of the best practices for supporting children as they make their way through the world of technology. These limits need to be informed by our own values and priorities for our children's flourishing and good health in the digital age – limits that balance safeguarding their welfare and sanctification while leaving the door open for them to experience its many human-enhancing benefits and joys.

1. Make a Family Tech Plan: Create a family technology plan that spells out specific rules for when, where and how your family uses technology. For instance, this could include planning maths homework for between 3pm and 5pm so that dinner is tech-free, or, planning for a family meeting or family devotions time to be tech-free; or, planning not looking at any devices 30 minutes before bedtime. Also, be sure the plan applies equally to the entire household so that your children can model tech habits after you.

2. Promote Healthy Use: Help your children balance their screen time with other activities to support their physical, emotional and spiritual wellbeing, such as outdoor play, family activities, reading and creative projects.

3. Monitor and curate content: Stay vigilant about the behaviour of your children online. Keep parental controls in place and utilise AI tools that filter for bad content, and regularly check in with whom they are sharing their content. Ask your children to show you what they are seeing and try to talk them through that content to teach them how to think critically about what they are encountering online.

4. Model Responsible Tech Use: Children are like sponges, so they will be bystanders, absorbing your behaviour. So, model responsible use of technology by using various media in a manner that honours God and respects others, and 'keep it real' by being open about your own struggles to manage your screen time, and your strategies for success in that regard.

Teaching Digital Discernment

Aside from safeguarding boundaries in this environment, Christian parents – who have a responsibility to shape their children in the ways of the Lord – must cultivate within them an ethic for media use, an ability to discern how to wield and use technology in ways that are ecologically and ethically appropriate to their faith.

1. Train your kids to be critical thinkers: Encourage your kids to ask questions about the content they view online: who wrote this? What is its message? Is it consistent with biblical principles? Teaching your children about discernment will help them become savvy consumers who will have a better sense of what is true and what is not.

2. Answer the question of online etiquette: Issues of online conduct also deserve discussion. Let your children know that, as in other areas of their lives, they should be kind, respectful, and honest in their online dealings, just as they are to those they meet in the 'real world'. Because they are siblings of someone in Jesus's family, they need to remain faithful in all things, including what they do online.

3 Cultivate a Heart for Others: Exalt character over fast thumbs. The culture in which your children are growing up heavily favours influence, visibility and power through social media. Although they're made in the image of God, this world teaches children that their worth is measured by the number of people who like, retweet, share or even read their latest post. Invite them to cultivate their influence online for others' good and encourage them to emulate you in becoming a force for Christ in their spaces.

4. Pray with Them About Their Digital Lives: Advocate prayer as a regular and natural part of digital life. Persuade teens to pray for wisdom about the God-honouring and respectful ways to use technology, and to intercede for others who are in difficult or dangerous situations online. Urge them to reflect on their tech use in light of their faith and values.

Creating a Tech-Positive Environment

Surely there is a role for limits and teaching discernment while still making it a rosy place, a tech-positive place that respects it as a powerful means of creativity, learning and community.

1. Seek Faith-Based Apps, Games, Media: Find faith-based apps, games and media that reinforce the values and doctrines of Christianity. There are many good learning tools that enhance children's faith and use technology for good, not evil purposes.

2. Embrace Technology: Technology may be a great in-road to connections: maintain contact with extended family via a video call; share family photos and memories online in a digital album; or play computer games together as a family for shared fun.

3. Teach Kids to Use Technology as a Tool: Give your children opportunities to use technology as a means of learning and creating. This could mean coding or digital art projects or exploring new knowledge in areas they're passionate about. Defining technology as a tool for learning more about God's creation and as a means of developing new abilities can help kids realise the full potential of technology.

Conclusion: Raising Tech-Savvy, Faith-Focused Children

You'll play your role of protecting your children from harmful technologies, and helping them have healthy limits, digital discernment and, most importantly, a good relationship with their devices. You will ensure that they take their cues from those models of healthy digital living you created while raising them, relying on your long-term vision, not the current soundbites their peers offer. Your kids will eventually thank you for guiding them through the digital jungle, with higher self-esteem and a fresh trust in technology.

We're raising kids for kingdom work; we want them fluent in technology, but with a heart for Jesus Our hope in Jesus informs our parenting strategies, and we do our best to structure our family's technology use with that perspective in mind. Raising kids for kingdom work, we want them fluent in technology, but with a heart for Jesus. With the right silver bullet, I'm convinced we can raise kids who use technology to glorify God and serve others. I can't tell you what that silver bullet is for sure, but it will include including faith in those kids' digital lives.

CHAPTER ELEVEN

AI in Worship: Enhancing Praise and Worship Experiences

Christianity emphasises the importance of worship, when believers unite in song to glorify God, reflect upon his good gifts, and confront his awesomeness in an epistemic, emotive and aesthetic experience, and ultimately encounter him. Today, AI is facilitating new ways to optimise this Christian experience, for it can make worship interactive, accessible and palatable. In this chapter, I explore how AI can be employed across music, liturgy, preaching and communal prayer to achieve a well-centred, calculated and Christ-centric worship.

AI and Worship Music

It has always helped Christians to touch God with their emotions and worship him, and they do that through music. AI is now musicians helping musicians enhance worship music in many creative ways.

1. New Worship Songs Composed by AI: AI can generate new worship songs that the worship leader or musician can then polish. An algorithm that has been trained on thousands of hymns, worship songs, and Psalms can autonomously compose a melody and lyrics to reflect the theological and emotional themes of this existing body of work. Human ingenuity and inspiration will never be replaced, but AI can serve as a muse or offer a creative reworking of beloved themes.

2. Personalised worship playlists for a given service or initiative, an AI system might provide a worship playlist, tailored to the needs of an individual worshipper, the theme of the service or the activity, or both. For instance, if the theme of a service is 'gratitude', the AI system might curate a playlist of musical works with lyrics that focus on thanksgiving and praise. They could use this to curate a deeper worship experience.

3. Real-Time Adaptive Music: Actual worship music could be adapted in real time to the energy level of the congregation, using AI. For example, AI systems could analyse the collective energy of the congregation via sound volume, movement or participation, and adjust the tempo, key or overall volume of the music more in tune with the worship service at a given point in time to increase the effectiveness of the service.

AI in Liturgy and Sermons

Liturgy and sermon are central to Christian worship, providing the framework for devotion, instruction and corporate reorientation. AI can amplify this effort in transformative ways:

1. Sermon Preparation and Delivery: AI can assist pastors in sermon preparation by providing relevant scriptural references, historical context, and theological insights. AI tools can also suggest ways to make sermons more engaging by analysing the structure, language, and delivery of previous sermons. While AI should never replace the spiritual guidance and discernment that pastors rely on, it can be a valuable resource in crafting messages that resonate with the congregation.

2. Interactive Liturgy: Given the adaptability of AI, such tools can also be used to make the liturgy more interactive for the congregants. For instance, AI-driven applications can provide real-time translations for non-native speakers, offer personalised reflections on the scriptures that one is reading, or even allow for virtual responses for the congregants online. This, in turn, provokes a more active participation for such congregants and could even be used in their home settings. This then makes the liturgy more accessible and allows for a more inclusive experience for the diverse membership of the congregation, especially for those in remote places.

3. Post-Sermon AI Commentary: AI can scrape congregational responses to a sermon (attention levels, quantity of notes taken, post-sermon questionnaires, etc) and provide pastors feedback on the effectiveness of the sermon, so that they can tweak it for future sermons and tailor the message to the wants and needs of the congregation.

Enhancing Communal Prayer with AI

Religious prayer is a deeply individual and communal divine service, and AI can support both the act of personal prayer and group prayer in multiple ways.

1. Prayer Matching and Support: AI systems could match people together during prayer according to prayer intentions/needs. For instance, an AI-powered app might match congregants who are praying about similar issues (such as healing or direction) so that they could pray together or support each other.

2. Guided Prayer Sessions: For those who struggle to maintain focus during prayers, online apps with AI-assisted guided prayer sessions could be especially beneficial. Such sessions can include readings from the Bible or other scriptures, reflections and prompts based on doctrinal principles, thus helping a believer concentrate on their prayers and stay faithful to their God.

3. Prayer Analytics: Prayer requests submitted by a congregation can provide valuable insight into the community's concerns. AI can be used by church leaders to analyse these requests, looking for common themes or urgent pastoral issues. This information can be used to influence the content area of prayers during worship services or to guide pastoral care programmes.

Balancing Innovation with Reverence

In many ways, AI opens a world of new possibilities for worship that I personally find exciting. But integration does not come without important considerations and a firm commitment to preserving the fragile worshipper. Here are some thoughts on engaging these technologies while creating ritual exposure that prioritises reverence.

1. 'Keep Christ in the Centre': AI assistance should always be a form of spiritual enhancement that supports Christ-centred worship, rather than distracting from the primary goal of worship – which is to glorify God and to draw us into a closer relationship with Jesus Christ.

2. Preserve Tradition: While innovation can bring much-needed new energy to the context of worship, it is imperative to retain the treasure trove of traditions that have become a part of our religious activities over centuries. AI can thereby complement not replace many timeless aspects of liturgy including the reading of scripture, the singing of hymns and the 'sacrament'.

3. Promote Participation, Not Spectatorship: AI should be used to enhance participation by congregants, not as means to turn them into passive observers. Worship is a community experience, and technology can further participation, whether by providing interactive liturgies, collective prayer or engaged music-making.

4. keeping it equitable and inclusive: AI will likely continue to be useful in building worship communities that include populations with disabilities, language barriers or geographical challenges, but they can also be used to limit access to certain individuals through digital or technological discrimination. We must be mindful to use our technologies in keeping with our commitment to open and inclusive worship practices.

Conclusion: Worshiping with Technology in Spirit and Truth

As such, I think that AI could enrich worship by making it more immersive or interactive, or by tailoring it to the individual more than purely human events can. But we need to be mindful, because, as with all technology, worship using AI will also require a commitment to maintaining sanctity and reverence to our interaction with God. If we allow it in, we do so with a commitment to creating sacred experiences, not mere diversion. By utilising AI, we can bring new, engaging ways of connecting with God into the framework of centuries-old worship, enriching the entire experience for the congregant.

In this search for possibility, we must proceed not with techno-egotism or a sense of self-s humility and discernment. We must ask whether such practices, however beautiful and brilliant, truly honour God and edify God's people along the way.

CHAPTER TWELVE

Christian Leadership and AI: Leading with Wisdom and Integrity

Christian leadership is not just about leading for the sake of leading but importantly about guiding others in their faith journey, helping them reach spiritual maturity and making decisions on behalf of disciples that reflect the life of Christ. The use of AI in leading people will pose challenges when it comes to modelling Christian leadership and therefore caring for others. This chapter considers how AI can aid Christian leadership. At the same time, it emphasises that Christian leadership is not about artificial intelligence but about wisdom and integrity infused by the spirit of Christ.

AI as a Tool for Decision-Making

Leadership is about making choices that affect others, whether it be leading a church, a Christian charity or wider community. AI can help leaders with these choices, by delivering – through data capture and analysis – snapshots, trends and foresight. Using AI-derived demographic data, church leaders will be able to make better choices regarding their congregants needs; and in broader communities, foresight regarding likely outcomes of given initiatives can be made – for instance, likely results of a locality extending an invitation to a new church in an area.

1. Data-Informed Decisions Issues of size and speed greatly favour the computer – it can analyse more data, faster than any human counterpart! And when it comes to running an effective ministry, more information often means better, mission-focused decisions. AI tools can be used to glean insight into congregation needs, assess attendance patterns, or to evaluate the impact of ministry programmes.

2. Scenario Planning: Based on a set of defined actions, AI can model scenarios, running through possible consequences of each path before the leader acts; this can be a useful aid in planning ahead for strategic purposes, in creating budgets and allocating resources, to help identify challenges and strengths.

3. Templated Intervention: AI will help pastors to scale their engagement with members of their community based on size or by looking at their web of relationships in a congregation. AI can do this analysis of interactions through attendance, participation habits and specific needs. This will allow leaders to speak to members with a focus on their interests and behaviours. The result will be more personalised pastoral care, discipleship and communication.

Ethical Considerations in AI-Driven Leadership

While AI offers many benefits, it also comes with ethical dilemmas that require a delicate balancing act by Christian leaders. The use of AI in leadership is predicated on the understanding that of all human beings, and therefore we need to be accountable and answerable to one another in ethical ways. Important Christian values such as justice, mercy and respect for the human person must be incorporated into how AI is used.

1. Transparency and accountability: Leaders must ensure that decisions made through AI are transparent and accountable. Making AI algorithmic models clear to those affected by them, offering explanations and justifying the data used to train them are just some of the transparency measures leaders can employ. Moreover, accountability contributes to the degree of transparency in leadership by making decisions traceable to the decision-makers on record. Accountability in this context is giving an account of the wellbeing and empowerment of the people for the way they are being governed by using AI. It can only be realised when decision-making becomes accountable to the people, and those at the receiving end of AI leadership can hold those leaders accountable. This can involve leaders being accountable to the people and adhering to the vision and teachings of Christ, their saviour and Redeemer.

2. Avoiding Over-Reliance on Technology: While AI can provide valuable insights, it should not replace the discernment and wisdom that come from prayer, reflection, and seeking God's guidance. Christian leaders must balance the use of AI with a reliance on the Holy Spirit, ensuring that their decisions are not solely based on data but are also informed by spiritual discernment.

3. Privacy and dignity: AI, as we've discussed, relies on using data, and probably also on analysing lots and lots of people's personal data. Leaders must make sure that those who are served or employed are given privacy and dignity so that the use of data is done ethically, with care to protect that privacy and dignity, and ensuring that people are not disadvantaged by systems that use such data. This includes, for instance, consent, data security and propriety, and sensitivity in the use of data in decision-making.

4. Promoting Justice and Fairness: AI systems can sometimes reflect and perpetuate biases, leading to unfair or discriminatory outcomes. Christian leaders must be proactive in identifying and addressing potential biases in AI tools, ensuring that decisions are just, equitable, and reflective of God's love for all people.

AI and Leadership Development

Alongside their work with their communities, Christian leaders are perhaps most responsible for cultivating new leaders. In this capacity, AI can support leadership development efforts by assisting with identifying potential leaders, delivering personalised training and developing more enhanced mentorship opportunities.

1. Leadership identification: Through pattern-detection of engagement, skills and behaviours, the AI can identify leadership emergent who show promise for future leadership positions. This information can help current leaders to see who might be emerging, and what support and development they can offer the individual to help the current leader grow their successor.

2. Personalised Leadership Training: Ai-based personalised learning programmes would create targeted activities (eg, online courses, reading materials and interactive simulations) to develop the key competencies of individual leaders according to their needs and strengths.

3. Mentorship and Networking: AI could connect senior leaders with those in training to offer mentorship and networking – an opportunity for emerging leaders to adopt best practices, build relationships, and develop their leadership capabilities.

Maintaining a Christ-Centered Focus in Leadership

It is also reflected in our approach to leadership in all its facets, where AI proves to be remarkably able. Complementary AI could assist in aligning God's calling in your life with your organisational purpose, as well as helping you realign when these objectives diverge. By orienting your leadership in a Christ-centred manner, you can attain humility, integrity and reliance upon God's wisdom for exceeding your personal competencies.

1. Prayerfully weighing alternatives: praying for guidance should form part of leaders' decision-making processes. AI can certainly help them find information or analyse data, but that should be seen as only one part of the broader spiritual or communal process.

2. Building a Servant Leadership Culture: Christians are called to serve; Jesus did not come to earth 'to be served but to serve', and so Christian leaders are called to be servants. AI can be used to enhance leaders' abilities to serve those whom they serve, not leaders' abilities to serve themselves.

3. Encouraging Participation: AI can help leaders to connect with their communities, but care must be taken so that leadership itself remains broad, participatory, and inclusive. Leaders should encourage dialogue and buy-in, and not just input, using AI as a tool to enable, not guide, decisions.

Conclusion: Leading with Integrity in an AI-Driven World

Christian leadership in the age of AI can be both scary and hopeful, problematic and powerful. Used rightly, with ethical intentionality and ongoing attention to ethical outcomes, AI might significantly enhance the capacity of church leaders to serve their communities, stand on truth, invest in future leaders, and enact an incarnational presence in the world. Used wrongly, or with a lack of commitment to transparency, accountability or a Christ-centred vision, the very same technologies could lead to all sorts of unethical behaviours, ruptures between leaders and constituents, and growing alienation among the larger church and the communities they are called to serve.

As Christian ministers and leaders, it is our responsibility to model wisdom, humility and integrity, to lead well and to continuously embody the love and teachings of Christ in order that AI can afford page breaks and hyphens thus better serving the cause of God's Kingdom and his people.

CHAPTER THIRTEEN

AI for Personal Growth: Leveraging Tech for Spiritual Development

In today's fast-paced world, personal and spiritual growth can sometimes feel like a challenge to maintain. However, with the advent of Artificial Intelligence (AI), new opportunities are emerging to support and enhance our spiritual development. This chapter explores how AI can be used as a tool for personal growth, helping Christians deepen their relationship with God, develop spiritual disciplines, and live out their faith in meaningful ways.

AI and Spiritual Disciplines

Spiritual disciplines such as prayer, Bible study, fasting, and meditation are essential practices for growing in faith. AI technology offers various tools to help believers cultivate these disciplines more effectively.

1. Personalized Bible Study Plans: AI-driven apps can create personalized Bible study plans based on your spiritual goals, current knowledge, and schedule. For example, if you are focused on understanding a particular book of the Bible or exploring themes like forgiveness or grace, AI can suggest specific passages, study guides, and resources that align with these interests. These tailored plans help ensure that your Bible study is both relevant and impactful.

2. Prayer Reminders and Journaling AI-powered apps can assist in maintaining a consistent prayer life by sending reminders to pray throughout the day and offering prompts for prayer journaling. These tools can help you track prayer requests, reflect on how God is answering prayers, and stay focused during your prayer time. Additionally, some apps use AI to suggest scriptures or meditations that complement your prayer life, making each session more enriching.

3. Guided Meditation and Reflection: Meditation on Scripture and reflection are vital for spiritual growth. AI can offer guided meditation sessions tailored to your needs, providing scripture-based reflections, calming music, or even breathing exercises that help you focus on God's Word. These sessions can be personalized based on your current spiritual state, whether you need encouragement, peace, or a deeper sense of connection with God.

Tracking and Measuring Spiritual Growth

One of the unique advantages of AI is its ability to track progress and provide insights over time. Just as fitness apps track physical health, AI-driven spiritual growth tools can help you monitor your spiritual journey, offering encouragement and guidance along the way.

1. Spiritual Growth Metrics: AI can analyse your engagement with spiritual practices, such as prayer, Bible reading, and church attendance, to provide feedback on your growth. For example, it might track how often you engage in Bible study, the diversity of the scriptures you read, or the consistency of your prayer life. These metrics can help you identify areas where you are thriving and areas where you might need more focus or support.

2. Personalized Growth Recommendations: Based on your tracked progress, AI can suggest next steps in your spiritual journey. If the data indicates that you've been consistently studying the Gospels, it might recommend exploring the Epistles for a broader understanding of New Testament teachings. Alternatively, if your prayer life has been more focused on personal requests, AI might suggest incorporating more intercessory prayer or prayers of thanksgiving.

3. Goal Setting and Accountability: AI can assist in setting spiritual goals and providing reminders and encouragement to help you achieve them. Whether your goal is to read through the Bible in a year, memorize scripture, or deepen your understanding of a particular theological concept, AI can create a customized plan and keep you accountable through regular check-ins.

Overcoming Challenges with AI

While AI offers many tools to support personal growth, it's important to recognize and address potential challenges that can arise from relying too heavily on technology.

1. Maintaining Authenticity: Spiritual growth is deeply personal and relational, involving your direct relationship with God. There is a risk that relying on AI could make your spiritual practices feel more like a checklist rather than a heartfelt pursuit. To maintain authenticity, it's crucial to use AI as a support tool rather than a replacement for genuine spiritual engagement. Ensure that your time with God remains intimate and sincere, guided by the Holy Spirit rather than solely by algorithms.

2. Avoiding Over-Dependence on Metrics: While tracking progress can be helpful, spiritual growth is not always measurable by data. The depth of your relationship with God cannot be fully captured by metrics. Be mindful not to become overly focused on numbers or achievements, but rather on the quality of your relationship with Christ and your responsiveness to His leading.

3. Balancing Technology with Silence and Solitude: Technology, even when used for spiritual growth, can sometimes become a distraction. It's important to balance the use of AI tools with time spent in silence and solitude, where you can listen to God without the interference of digital devices. These moments of quiet reflection are essential for hearing God's voice and discerning His will.

Integrating AI into Daily Life

To effectively leverage AI for personal growth, it's important to integrate these tools into your daily routine in a way that complements your existing spiritual practices.

1. Start Small: Begin by incorporating one or two AI-driven tools into your routine. For example, you might start with an AI-powered Bible study app and a prayer reminder tool. As you become more comfortable with these tools, you can gradually explore other options that support your spiritual goals.

2. Stay Connected to Community: While AI can enhance personal growth, spiritual development is also deeply communal. Make sure to stay connected to your church, small groups, or Christian mentors who can provide guidance, encouragement, and accountability. Share your experiences with AI tools, but also seek the wisdom and support of others in your faith community.

3. Regularly Evaluate and Adjust Periodically to assess how AI is

impacting your spiritual growth. Are the tools helping you deepen your relationship with God? Are they encouraging you to engage more fully with scripture, prayer, and service? If you find that certain tools are becoming more of a distraction than a help, don't hesitate to adjust your approach or even take a break from technology altogether.

Conclusion: AI as a Partner in Spiritual Growth

Artificial Intelligence offers exciting possibilities for enhancing personal and spiritual growth, providing tools that can help you stay connected to God, develop spiritual disciplines, and track your progress. However, it's essential to use these tools thoughtfully, ensuring that they serve as a support rather than a replacement for genuine, heartfelt engagement with your faith.

By integrating AI into your spiritual practices with discernment and intentionality, you can leverage technology to grow closer to God, deepen your understanding of His Word, and live out your faith in ways that are both meaningful and transformative.

CHAPTER FOURTEEN

Evangelism in the Digital Age: Spreading the Gospel with AI

T he Great Commission—Jesus' command to go and make disciples of all nations—remains the central mission of the Christian faith. In the digital age, the methods of evangelism are evolving, and Artificial Intelligence (AI) is opening new avenues for spreading the Gospel. This chapter explores how AI can be utilized to share the message of Christ with a global audience, offering strategies for effective digital evangelism while ensuring that the integrity of the Gospel is upheld.

AI-Powered Evangelism Tools

AI technology offers a variety of tools that can assist in evangelistic efforts, making it possible to reach people in ways that were previously unimaginable.

1. Targeted Outreach: AI can analyse data from social media, search engines, and online forums to identify individuals who may be open to hearing the Gospel. By recognizing patterns in online behaviour, AI can help evangelists target their outreach to those who are seeking spiritual answers or who have expressed interest in Christian topics. This targeted approach can make evangelism more effective by connecting with people where they are most receptive.

2. Chatbots and Virtual Assistants: AI-powered chatbots and virtual assistants can engage in conversations with individuals seeking answers about faith, Christianity, and the meaning of life. These chatbots can provide instant responses to common questions, share Bible verses, or guide users to local churches or online resources. While human evangelists are irreplaceable, AI can serve as an initial point of contact, offering timely and accessible information.

3. Content Creation and Distribution: AI can assist in creating and distributing evangelistic content, such as articles, videos, and social media posts. By analysing what types of content resonate with different audiences, AI can help craft messages that are more likely to engage and inspire. Additionally, AI can automate the distribution of content across multiple platforms, ensuring that the message of the Gospel reaches a broader audience.

Reaching the Unreached

One of the most significant opportunities AI presents is the ability to reach people who have never heard the Gospel. In areas where traditional missionary efforts are challenging due to geographical, cultural, or political barriers, AI can help bridge the gap.

1. Language Translation: AI-driven language translation tools can help overcome language barriers, making it possible to share the Gospel with people who speak different languages. These tools can translate written content, subtitles for videos, or even live conversations, allowing for more effective communication with diverse populations.

2. Localized Evangelism: AI can analyse cultural and social trends in specific regions to tailor evangelistic messages that resonate with local audiences. By understanding the values, beliefs, and concerns of different communities, evangelists can present the Gospel in a way that is culturally relevant and respectful.

3. Digital Mission Fields: The internet itself is a vast mission field, with millions of people searching for answers to life's biggest questions. AI can help identify these digital seekers, providing opportunities for evangelists to engage with them through online forums, social media, and dedicated evangelistic websites.

Challenges and Ethical Considerations in AI-Driven Evangelism

While AI offers powerful tools for evangelism, it also raises important challenges and ethical considerations that must be carefully navigated.

1. Maintaining Authenticity: One of the risks of AI-driven evangelism is the potential for messages to become impersonal or overly automated. The Gospel is a deeply personal message of love, grace, and redemption, and it's essential that this authenticity is not lost in the process. Evangelists should ensure that AI is used to enhance, not replace, personal interactions and relationships.

2. Respecting Privacy: AI's ability to analyse and target individuals based on their online behaviour raises concerns about privacy. It's important to use these tools responsibly, ensuring that people's data is handled with care and respect. Evangelists should be transparent about how data is used and avoid intrusive or manipulative tactics.

3. Avoiding Cultural Insensitivity: AI-driven evangelism must be culturally sensitive and respectful. While AI can help tailor messages to different audiences, it's crucial to ensure that the Gospel is presented in a way that honours local customs and beliefs. Evangelists should seek to understand the cultural context and work collaboratively with local believers to share the message of Christ in a way that is both meaningful and appropriate.

Best Practices for AI-Driven Evangelism

To effectively use AI in evangelism, consider the following best practices:

1. Integrate AI with Human Effort: AI should complement, not replace, human evangelistic efforts. Use AI to enhance your reach and efficiency but ensure that personal relationships and face-to-face interactions remain central to your approach.

2. Focus on Relational Evangelism: While AI can help initiate conversations and provide information, it's essential to move beyond digital interactions to build genuine relationships. Follow up with those who express interest in the Gospel, offering to meet in person, connect through video calls, or introduce them to a local church community.

3. Train and Equip Digital Evangelists: Ensure that those using AI tools for evangelism are well-trained and equipped to handle the challenges of digital ministry. This includes understanding the technology, ethical considerations, and best practices for sharing the Gospel online.

4. Pray for Guidance and Wisdom: As with any form of ministry, prayer is essential. Seek God's guidance in how to use AI effectively and ethically in evangelism. Pray for wisdom in reaching out to others, and for the Holy Spirit to work through these efforts to bring people to faith in Christ.

Conclusion: Spreading the Gospel in a Digital World

AI offers unprecedented opportunities to spread the Gospel, reaching people across the globe in ways that were once unimaginable. However, it is crucial that these tools are used with integrity, respect, and a deep commitment to the message of Christ.

By integrating AI into evangelism with discernment and a focus on building authentic relationships, we can harness technology to fulfil the Great Commission, bringing the hope of the Gospel to those who need it most. As we navigate this new frontier, let us do so with faith, creativity, and a steadfast commitment to sharing the love of Christ with the world.

CHAPTER FIFTEEN

Balancing Tech Use: Ensuring AI Serves Your Faith, Not Distracts from It

As we find ourselves in an age of Artificial Intelligence (AI) and accelerated technological innovations, the stakes of faith for Christians are arguably higher than ever since we must ask how do we employ AI and other technological tools to further our humanity, love God, engage in spiritual practices, and serve others, while avoiding the horizons and pitfalls that this latest human invention creates for the distinctives of a Christ-centred life?

This chapter of the book underscores the essential aspects of balance when it comes to tech use, especially not how AI can distract us from, but rather enrich and nourish our faith, while sharing some helpful ideas and suggestions for implementing practical guidelines that can keep technology useful and not detrimental. Read More ›

The Temptation of Distraction in a Digital World

The continual connectivity of the digital age also carries its own risks: a relentless series of AI-driven algorithms pushing notifications to capture our attention and keep us hooked to social media, entertainment or e-commerce apps, or merely hours of browsing. Perhaps more than ever, the tools designed to make our lives easier risk pulling us in directions that we had no intention of moving towards.

For instance, AI algorithms found on platforms such as YouTube or Facebook are built to recommend to us more content that we're likely to personally enjoy. This kind of recommendation can facilitate learning and advancement in certain situations, but it can also develop into an unhealthy habit of endless consumption, where we endlessly 'consume our way up the food chain'. One video after another, one article after another, is 'suggested' when we certainly didn't request it and rarely ties into the crux of the content that we first landed on with a spiritual intention, such as the search for insight into our daily lives that seek to promote ever greater spirituality. If we're not careful, before we know it, we've spent an hour of endless 'content consumption', finding very little in the way of nourishment for our spiritual journey.

This is not to suggest that there is anything inherently wrong with technology or AI, but rather that, if these tools are not used with care and discernment, they can keep us from engaging in good spiritual practices and even manipulate us into bad ones. Ample examples of this are now emerging. When done well, AI tools can enhance Bible study, prayer and ministry outreach, but we need to be aware of this so that we are using targeting and engagement tools for Kingdom purposes, not the other way around.

AI as a Tool, not a Master

Which leads to the next step: to make sure that AI works for your faith, you must recognise that AI is simply a tool. It's a means to an end, not an end. You use it to get you somewhere – just like you use several other tools or instruments for so many different parts of your daily life and personal needs (a car to get places; a calendar app to keep track of time; meditation for your spiritual practice; a tattoo for your spiritual expression).

Therefore, it would be beneficial to establish boundaries around the how and when of technology (for instance, through limiting the screen time; scheduling periods of routine, tech-free rituals such as prayer and reflection; choosing to read the right kinds of content, etcetera). In terms of securing the role of AI as a servant versus master, the onus is just as much on us as it is on the capabilities of AI.

Cultivating Digital Discernment

One of the most valuable skills we can cultivate for our digital life is discernment: the ability to distinguish what is edifying from what is distracting, or even destructive. Just as we strive to discern truth and false life, so must we tech use.

The algorithms that make such suggestions learn more about us – what will keep us on a site – and the more we click, the more we are served with stories, opinions or anything else that fits our habitual ('addictive') patterns of action. This is so convenient, but it also means we get stuck in an echo chamber giving us less and less exposure to others, particularly in the public square, in a way that enables meaningful dialogue. How can we grow in Christ-like agape love, character and conduct in a life where we don't even see straight?

What do we need instead? More intentionality about what we read and above all, purposeful choices about how we relate to technology: 1. Every time we grab a device, ask ourselves what we hope to get out of it. And then exit and ask if we accomplished that purpose.2. Seek technologies that let us engage meaningfully with the media we consume.3. At the end of each week, make intentional choices about how you'll engage with technology over the coming week. Decide what kind of media you'll visit and how much   engaging only with trusted sources you've selected for quality, for instance, and setting aside time for news and information.

1. Judge based on content through a faith lens: Ask yourself before you begin: is my spirit ready to engage with this content (whatever it is, be it a video, an article, a social media post, etc)? Is it going to contribute to my development as a believer and help me live out my faith more richly? Is it true, is it edifying? Is it something I need to see right now? If not, then perhaps skip.

2. Find Different Voices: The advantages of following these guidelines would include keeping biblical truth at the centre of what we seek and read online, while at the same time taking advantage of the diverseness of our human experience so that we can engage Christian brothers and sisters who think and believe differently from us. Sometimes, bots – much like preachers and professors – will simply affirm our views, so it is worth the time to find those voices in the digital space that will challenge your faith in ways that stretch and expand the horizons of your walk with God.

3. Reduce Exposure to Things That Breed Negativity, Division or Fear: The digital world is filled with content full of negativity, discord, and fear. As Christians, we are to 'make every effort to keep the unity of the Spirit through the bond of peace' (Ephesians 4:3) and to build others up according to our 'measures' gifted to us by God (Ephesians 4:29). If you find that you are angry, frustrated or fearful after timing yourself or listening to certain political debates, news or social media spats, consider limiting your use of such media.

Establishing Boundaries for Healthy Tech Use

But if we're going to put faith into AI, the first step should be to implement healthier contexts for our tech use: clear boundaries around apps help us avoid letting technology dominate our reason and time, which ultimately robs us of our capacity to give God, family and community their due.

Here are some practical steps for establishing boundaries:

1. Make God-Gab Time Device-Free: Pick specific seasons each day for device-free gab time with God. Your morning devotional, before bed or at your mealtime can be these occasions. In fact, praying when you're driving alone is a great way to remind yourself to stay fully present in the moment, so you are better able to engage yourself at the computer or behind the wheel.

2. AI should be a Helper, not a Replacement for Spiritual Practices: Many AI-powered apps exist to help us research the Bible, pray or prepare our devotions. They can be helpful tools to supplement our spiritual practices. However, these new technology solutions should supplement and assist, not dominate or replace our personal, intimate relationship with God. Digital tools should help us deepen our walk with God and should never be a substitute for directly engaging with our Bibles, in prayer or in worship.

3. Establish Tech-Free Zones: Set up certain areas of your home or specific periods of the zones, such as the dinner table, the bedroom, or family devotional time. Doing so facilitates more authentic human-to-human connections and ensures that you keep your attention where it matters the most.

4. Reduce Multitasking: Multitasking is another 'full-throttle spot' for distraction – especially where tech is involved. So, if you're using an AI-enhanced Bible study app, or communicating with God through an AI-based prayer app: don't be tempted to engage in other activities at the same time. Don't check emails or scroll through social media while you are using an AI Bible app or prayer app. Don't attempt to text or participate in a Zoom call while you're praying with an AI prayer app. Try to do one thing at a time.

5. Impose Time Limits on Digital Consumption: Many devices and apps have built-in features where one can set a time limit on certain digital activities (e.g. the use of social media- or entertainment-related apps). Impose such a limit on your devices and apps and allow yourself to restrict your time spent on the digitally consumed elements of your day.

Fostering Community and Accountability

Beyond the importance of individual self-discipline, a positive form of self-surveillance can also be valuable in community and in relationship with others. To use technology properly, we can benefit from the humbling practices that foster our own accountability. Just as we depend on Christian community to help our spiritual wellbeing, we likewise depend on others' guidance for managing technology so that we may maintain our own balance.

1. Form or Join a Tech Accountability Group: Find a few people at your church or in your community who are willing to form or join a small group together, where you could share how you are doing with technology each week. People could share the challenges that they are encountering, share helpful resources, and hold each other accountable on staying balanced.

2. Bring Tech Conversations into Family Life: If you are part of a family, bring regular tech conversations into family life so everyone can talk about tech use. Talk about how everyone is role modelling balance towards each other, set collective goals to reduce screen time, and encourage each other to put faith and relationships before digital distractions.

3. Model behaviour: If you are a parent, big sister or big brother, youth pastor or church leader, young people are looking at you to see what you do with your phone. Model tech habits that nourish you and demonstrate to others that AI can be a tool for spiritual growth, rather than a distraction.

Conclusion: Embracing AI with Intention and Faith

This tendency exists in a digital world where it can be difficult to be more discerning, to manage healthy boundaries, and to keep Jesus in the centre of our digital lives. So, in this, and all else, strive towards the middle way. Make AI be your servant, not your master. Give it a place, but let your faith be in Jesus, not technology.

With society increasingly shaped by digital technology, it's critical to keep in mind that technological innovations are gifts from God; they exist to advance God's Kingdom and to glorify God. When using AI as a creative agent, we can set our technological tools toward that end, and consciously use their power to better glorify God through a life shaped by faith. Prayerfully employing AI can help 'scale up' human potential towards its God-given forearms. Atheists may still be sceptical. But perhaps praying or making the Sign of the Cross after changing a value on a spreadsheet or a data table won't seem so strange when you're collaborating with the very qualities of the Creator who imbued you and your machine with eternity.

CHAPTER SIXTEEN

Planning for the Days Ahead: 'Let Your Light Shine and Shine Before All Men'

With every passing year, deep into the 21st century like we are deeply into it now, the world of Artificial Intelligence (AI) infiltrates deeper and deeper into our lives in ways no one could have predicted even 10 years ago. The rate of change is increasing. New opportunities, arise. The future is upon us, and for Christians, it's about embracing it – both the opportunities and the uncertainties of living and sharing Jesus in the AI world to come. The future is about ensuring that Christ is centre, and that AI-powered life is lived as not just another way to do whatever it is we think we are here to do, but that it does so as Jesus requires.

The Expanding Role of AI in Society

AI has already insinuated itself into almost every part of our modernity: from consent forms and school curricula to sales pitches and binge-viewing platforms, AI systems are making decisions, shaping experiences and automating the world's drudge work. And within a decade, AI likely will extend its reach over nearly every communication, learning, working, commuting and worshipping experience that most people have.

In the marketplace, AI will likely continue to redefine industries on the road to more efficient operations, increased automation, predictive insights, and all that. In the healthcare field, AI can potentially revolutionise treatment and diagnosis, ultimately saving lives by detecting diseases early on. In the educational sector, AI-powered tools can help students learn at their own pace with customised delivery of knowledge, so that their true potential can be unlocked. For the Church, AI provides opportunities for more targeted ministry, more expansive evangelism, and more deliberate engagement with people all around the world.

Even so, with such advancements will follow the inevitable questions: how do we ethically utilise AI? How does it factor into our personal and spiritual lives? And, perhaps most importantly, how do we work towards embracing a future, not all that far away, where AI is further embedded into the fundamental experience of our daily lives – all while keeping Jesus at the centre?

AI and Spiritual Growth: Tools for Tomorrow's Disciples

One of the most exciting prospects for the use of AI is in the realm of spiritual wellbeing. AI aids are already helping believers with routine spiritual practice – think of those apps that act as a study bible, with customised passages selected just for you, apps that remind you to pray or meditate, and guides for navigating the spiritual life. Over time, these AI tools will only improve in sophistication, giving believers even more ways to feel connected to and supported by their own faith.

For example, a Bible study might be far more rich and vivid in an AI-enhanced scenario – allowing users to, say, dive in and explore scripture in virtual or augmented reality, and uncover new or deeper aspects of its contexts and themes. AI might prompt a user with scripture, prayer or other reflections tailored to their life settings and spiritual needs.

Nonetheless, a sincere and truthful consumer of AI technologies adept at spiritual formation must never lose sight of the fact that, while strengthening our relationship with God, AI can never, for a self-aware Christian, replace it. AI will always have to be supplemental to faith, continually oriented toward engaging with Christ, never becoming a replacement that disconnects us from Him.

Ethical AI: Upholding Christian Values in a Digital World

As AI continues to grow more powerful, striving for the proper ethical use of AI will be a task with growing significance for Christians. AI systems are prone to mirroring human prejudices. They can lead to privacy violations or outcomes that generate tangible harm for individuals and their communities without proper safeguards. As Christians, we are to 'do justice, and to love kindness, and to walk humbly with our God' (Micah 6:8). This extends to advocating for viable and equitable AI technologies.

Here, the Christian community can play a leading role in developing the moral imagination necessary to shape the use of AI in ethical ways. This means agreeing on and promoting government policy and company practice aimed at effective and just AI use, including attention to racial and other forms of discrimination. And it is essential that Christian ethics, rooted in the human being as a Creature of God, remain central to these discussions. This is an opportunity for us to fulfil the commandment to 'love your neighbour as yourself'.

AI must be developed and implemented in accordance with human dignity, the common good, and justice. Christians can be ambassadors for these principles by encouraging the development of AI that embodies Christ's love and compassion for all.

AI in Ministry and Evangelism: Expanding God's Kingdom

In a way, the most promising developments in the future of AI will primarily exist to expand the scope and multitude of ministry and evangelistic opportunities. By analysing social media and other big data, AI can zero in on those searching online for spiritual answers or facing a crisis and allow one to 'pray' about when that person digs into issues or experiences a sense of God calling to him or her. AI-powered chatbots and virtual assistants can converse with seekers and provide scripture, answers and directions to the nearest church or online community.

AI could also open worship to those who for whatever reason – illness, disability or geographical distance – are unable to participate in physical spaces/services. In this way, AI could be a tool for equality. Many AI tools can be used to participate in virtual worship and engage in Bible studies for the 'church'.

Even if that day ever does come, human evangelism and ministry will ultimately still be about sharing the love of Christ toward others and building relationships within the context of a group. What AI will do and is doing is only to help us expand our reach, not to necessarily displace the need for those personal and human elements, nor the compassion and care, empathy and love that discipleship often demands of us.

Preparing for the Future: How Christians Can Lead the Way

For Christians, this future might offer a special vocation for an age of AI: if we desire to be leaders in the technological future, it will be as Christians above all else. How might we prepare for such a future so that whatever comes remains faithful to our calling?

1. Stay In Touch with Scripture and Prayer: In a rapidly evolving world, we need to stay in touch with what will never change: the truths of God's Word. Both Scripture and prayer will be the rudder that keeps us on course, that helps us discern how we should use AI and how it will use us when it comes to making decisions about the future.

2. Form an ecosystem for biblical thinking about technology: As more robust AI becomes a reality; Christians must also create a biblical framework for technology: What should be our public stance concerning technology? How can we steer AI policies toward shaping a world that better embodies biblical values? How can we utilise AI to promote the kingdom of God?

3. Talking points: Christians need to take part in AI ethics discussions. We should do this both with software developers to set parameters for the use of AI, and with other stakeholders such as policymakers and the public, to establish meaningful metrics for human flourishing. We should push back against opacity, discrimination and the infringement of human dignity in all AI applications.

4. Nurture Vibrant Community and Accountability: Finally, the embrace of AI in our lives must also be bound up in our Christian community, finding expression in the shared life with other Christians. Feeding off one another in fellowship and sharing the journey, being held accountable to walk 'circumspectly', allowing other Christians to help us find ways to check our own technological habits to reinforce our walk with Jesus and to maintain our relationships with God and our brothers and sisters as the primary expressions of the rest of our lives.

Be a Witness for Christ in the Digital World: As the world of AI continues to grow, so does our opportunity for being a witness for Christ in the digital world. Whether through online evangelism and digital ministry, or even just in our interactions on social media and spaces, AI can help us to share the Gospel and show the love of Christ to those who do not yet know Him.

Conclusion: Keeping Christ at the Centre

Now, as we, belatedly, enter this new era of technological potentiality blended with fear, Christian responses must be thoughtful, intentional, and prayerful. There's much to anticipate as well as much to contend with as we ride out the crests and endure the troughs of a new technological tsunami. AI is just a tool like all others, whether for good or ill. We will have to do our best to use it well. Originally published in Christianity Today.

In this way, keeping Christ at the centre of our activity in this new place means that we can journey because we are called to be custodians of creation as well as witnesses to God's deemed love. In so doing, we can use AI as an instrument of God's Kingdom, readying ourselves and others for the future by faithfulness, wisdom and fidelity to the Gospel.

Conclusion: Embracing AI with Faith, Wisdom, and Integrity

Standing at this intersection of hope and worry, it is undeniable that AI presents substantial opportunities and threats for Christians. This book has mapped out some of the ways in which AI might be integrated within a Christ-centred life, not only enhancing our spiritual engagement, aiding ministry, and extending the proclamation of the Gospel, but also helping us to live that Gospel out in our daily lives. As we move into the future, we must do so in faith, but also in wisdom and integrity.

The Promise of AI in a Christian Life

AI can provide us with tools that help us grow closer to God, connect more with other believers, and serve others more effectively. Let's explore a select number of these opportunities.

1. Applied Bible principles in AI technologies: Bible scholars are developing AI-based technologies that can 'think' like a biblical writer and allow us to apply principles from the Bible to various situations we encounter in daily life.

2. Personalised prayer: AI can help us identify and talk to God about issues and sins that might otherwise remain undetected.

3. Leadership: AI can be a friend to the leadership in the Church. Through sentiment and tone analysis, an AI might be able to identify and nurture the leadership gifts of individuals within a church. Locating and nurturing these gifts could lead to a healthier and more spiritually fruitful church.

4. Evangelism: If we accepted intelligent AI as our friend, then it could be effective in leading others to faith. AI could respond to people's spiritual questions in a way that makes them more comfortable in approaching a Christian with further enquiries.

These will all help us adhere to our disciplines of the spirit, help us better understand our Bibles, and better reach those otherwise unreachable. Worship can be made more accessible and inclusive, ministry can be more efficient and cost-effective, and sanctification more trackable and measurable. Believers can be connected like never before across countries and cultures, enabling virtual communities where those in the digital kingdom can more tangibly love God and one another.

Navigating the Ethical Challenges

There benefits to using AI, but doing so will raise ethical issues too. As Christians, we may be open to the ways in which technology can enhance our ability to be faithful citizens and human beings. However, lest we forget, we are called to be a movement of justice and fairness, and we must be sure every aspect of our lives – including the use of technology – trains us to respect the dignity of others as our neighbours.

With AI proved to be able to move people's behaviour, to make decisions for them, or process immense amounts of information about them, what happens to their privacy? What happens to their autonomy? Who will we hold accountable? We must ensure that AI is used in a manner that respects the dignity of every person, to strive for fairness and inclusion, and to safeguard the weakest among us. This means always watching for the insidious encroachment of bias, making certain that we have mechanisms of transparency in place, and that there are adequate guidelines regarding what is ethical and what is not, and always privileging people over technology – not just when it comes to efficiency, but also profit.

Maintaining a Christ-Cantered Focus

This theme of keeping Christ preeminent in all things, even in our use of AI kits, continues to recur throughout the book. Technology should never replace our relationship with God, our commitment to living according to God's Word, or our service to others.

AI can enhance and supplement our prayer practices, but it should never replace the lived availability – the heart-engaged prayerfulness – at the centre of a Christian life. The same is true of all our engagements with God and with one another: Holy Spirit-guided time spent in prayer, worship, and learning, and love-informed relationships with other human beings, not determined by algorithms.

With AI increasingly embedded in our society, it will be important to be continually asking: Is this tool making me a better disciple of Christ? Does it help me live more like Jesus? Does it help me love and serve my neighbour better? Christ will remain to the centre of our technology, and our technology will help us build God's Kingdom, and not allow us to become distracted from it.

The Role of Christian Community

This difficult work of bringing AI under a Christ-shaped horizon does not have to be done alone. In community, we can talk through the issues our technologies raise, share our frustrations and victories, and encourage each other in holding our AI accountable to God.

Churches, small groups and Christian organisations need to be a step ahead, providing a voice on the issue, guidance for believers, and resources for mistakes and challenges. And together we can imagine ways to use AI to make our communities stronger and more effective in supporting our ministry and extending God's love to those who have yet come to know it.

Looking to the Future with Hope and Caution

What is coming is undoubtedly this: life will be more and more suffused with AI. From that point onwards, the speed of development will only increase. What is coming is far wider, deeper, more subtle, more intimate – more ubiquitous finally – than anything that has come before. As Christians, we ought to meet the future with both a sense of cautious hope and of deep concern.

Hope, knowing that God rules over all things under heaven – yes, including technology. God can use AI for His glory, to generate further opportunities to bring the Gospel, to build the kingdom, to promote justice, to cultivate human flourishing; and caution, knowing that God would have us steward well the technologies and tools he places in our hands so that they're used for purposes He wills.

A Final Charge

I hope that, as you put down this book, you'll find yourself thinking about new ways that AI could be part of your life so that it might bring glory to God. How could you use it to deepen your walk with God, to love your neighbour, and to live into your faith online?

But AI is only a tool. The true power of our faith comes from our relationship with Christ, from how we love others, from the hope of the Gospel. Use it wisely. Use it prayerfully. Use it with discernment and integrity. Use it in glory to God.

With so many doorways opening and closing in this evolving world, may we stay faithful, open and present to what God is doing, both within us and beyond us. May we embrace technologically evolution to the glory of God and the honour of Christ; to be found faithful to the Word that remains steadfast and true, and to walk by faith amid the incredible possibilities offered by AI. Amen.

'Now may the God of peace... make you perfect in every good work to do his will, working in you that which is well pleasing in his sight, through Jesus Christ; to him be glory for ever and ever. Amen.' (Hebrews 13:20-21, NIV)

PART II

Selected Books by the Author

These books can be viewed/ bought by following the link below to the Amazon site:

https://selvasmail.com/selvasbooks

Alternatively, should you wish to view the books on your phone or tablet, you could scan the bar-code below, which will also take you direct to the Amazon site.

Scan me

BOOKS ON WELLNESS & HEALTH (7 BOOKS)

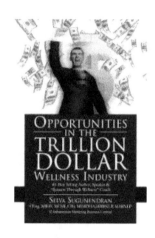

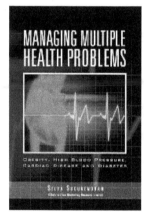

BOOKS ON ALZHEIMER'S DEMENTIA (6 BOOKS)

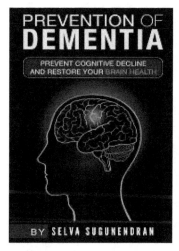

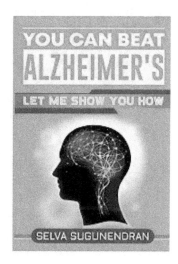

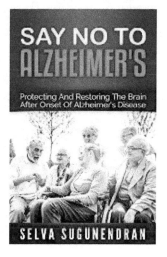

BOOKS ON SUCCESS (5 Books)

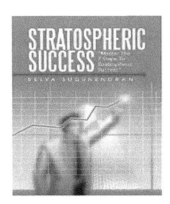

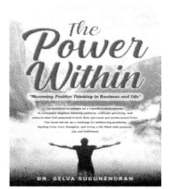

AI ROBOTICS (7 BOOKS)

CHRISTIAN BOOKS (18 BOOKS)

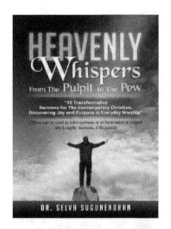

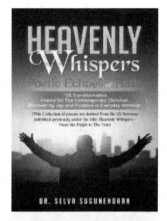

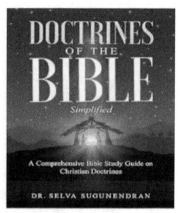

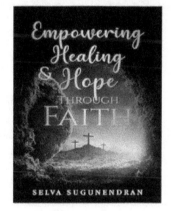

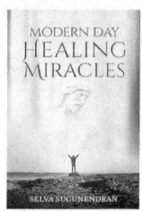

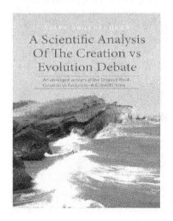

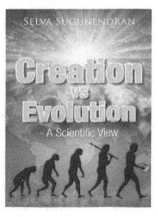

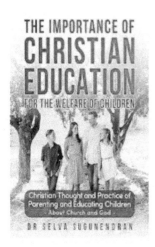

THE IMPORTANCE OF
CHRISTIAN
EDUCATION
FOR THE WELFARE OF CHILDREN

Christian Thought and Practice of
Parenting and Educating Children
- About Church and God -

DR SELVA SUGUNENDRAN

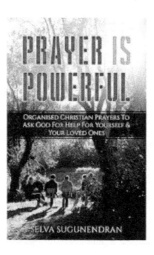

PRAYER IS
POWERFUL

ORGANISED CHRISTIAN PRAYERS TO
ASK GOD FOR HELP FOR YOURSELF &
YOUR LOVED ONES

SELVA SUGUNENDRAN

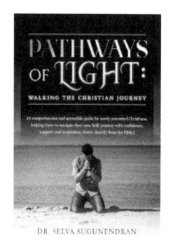

PATHWAYS
OF LIGHT:
WALKING THE CHRISTIAN JOURNEY

DR. SELVA SUGUNENDRAN

A LIVE DEBATE
AMONGST 3 YOUNG SCIENTISTS
On Eight Key Areas of Evolution

SELVA SUGUNENDRAN

21 REASONS
Why Evolution Lacks Scientific Proof

SELVA SUGUNENDRAN

BIG BANG
THEORY DEMYSTIFIED

SELVA SUGUNENDRAN

THE
POWER OF DIVINE
CONVERSATIONS
UNLOCKING THE SECRETS OF PRAYER

DR. SELVA SUGUNENDRAN

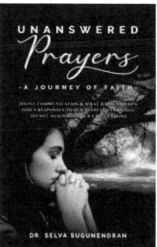

UNANSWERED
Prayers
- A JOURNEY OF FAITH -

DR SELVA SUGUNENDRAN

BELIEF
BEYOND
BOUNDARIES:
EMBRACING THE EXTRAORDINARY
THROUGH CHRISTIAN FAITH

By
DR. SELVA SUGUNENDRAN

APPENDICES

1.   **WEBSITE LINKS**

https://AIRoboticsForGood.com

https://MyChristianLifestyle.org

https://BlessMeLord.com

https://HealMeLord.today

https://CreationEvolutionAndScience.com

https://AIRoboticsForGood.com

https://DementiaAdvice.care

https://HowToLeadAVibrantLifeWithAlzheimers.com

2. CONTACT LINKS:

The Author Email: Selva@MyChristianLifestyle.org

All Books by Author Available on Amazon:

https://selvasmail.com/selvasbooks

www.ingramcontent.com/pod-product-compliance
Lightning Source LLC
LaVergne TN
LVHW081529050326
832903LV00025B/1704